Cultivating Readers

Everything you need to take reading instruction beyond the skills to addressing the will

ANNE ELLIOTT

MARY LYNCH

Pembroke Publishers Limited

Dedications:

To Charmaine Graves – Leader, Mentor, and Friend. —A.E. & M.L.

To my parents, Jim and Mary Elliott, the greatest reading models a child could ever have; my sister Kate, aka my book buddy for life; and my brother John, who is insatiably curious about our world and is a true wilful reader. A complete family of readers! —A. E.

To my husband Peter, thank you for humoring my passion for books and tolerating my countless Amazon deliveries; to my children Mark and Jennifer you will forever be my favorite students and readers; and to my Dad, Joseph "Dan" Kenney: Yes, it is finally done! —M.L.

538 Hood Road
Markham, Ontario, Canada L3R 3K9
www.pembrokepublishers.com

Distributed in the U.S. by Stenhouse Publishers
PO Box 11020
Portland, ME 04104-7020
www.stenhouse.com

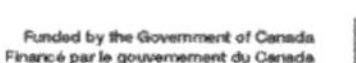

Library and Archives Canada Cataloguing in Publication

Elliott, Anne E. (Anne Elizabeth), author
Cultivating readers : 6 essential steps to foster the will to read / Anne Elliott & Mary Lynch.

Issued in print and electronic formats.
ISBN 978-1-55138-324-8 (softcover).--ISBN 978-1-55138-926-4 (PDF)

1. Reading (Elementary). 2. Reading promotion. I. Lynch, Mary, 1962–, author II. Title.

LB1573.E45 2017 372.41 C2017-903699-8
C2017-903700-5

Editor: Kat Mototsune
Cover Design: John Zehethofer
Typesetting: Jay Tee Graphics Ltd.

Printed and bound in Canada
9 8 7 6 5 4 3 2 1

Contents

Chapter 4: Third Step: Modeling the Habits of a Reader *50*

Chapter 5: Fourth Step: Making the *Why* of Reading Visible *84*

Introduction: Answering the Call

I ask those of you who are truly concerned about reading instruction to become my partners in igniting a passion for reading in schools. I ask you to raise your voices in faculty meetings and college classrooms, in literacy conferences and at parent nights and educate people about aliteracy—the "invisible liquid seeping through our culture." And then… offer your listeners hope, ideas, and solutions for change.

— Steven Layne, *Igniting a Passion for Reading* (p. 13)

Books have power. They have the ability to inspire, motivate, encourage, move, and change their readers. For years as teachers we have invested in refining our craft through professional reading, studying various books about creating a skilful reader. We worked diligently to ensure our instruction addressed phonetics, fluency, semantics, syntax, and comprehension. We were led by the work of Pearson et al., Harvey & Goudvis, Keene & Zimmerman, Gear, and others, all who revolutionized our understanding of reading and what proficient readers do, as they identified and labeled the thinking strategies consistently used by proficient readers as they make meaning from text (i.e., activating background knowledge, making connections to schema, questioning, visualizing, inferring, determining important ideas, synthesizing). It was as if Harry Potter himself had lifted the invisibility cloak and allowed us to see for the first time the invisible actions that take place in the reader's brain. Reading research changed our understanding, not only as reading teachers, but also as readers ourselves. We suddenly became acutely aware of the active thinking that was taking place in our own heads as we engaged with text. To be considered a skilful reader, you have to demonstrate an ability to monitor your comprehension while you read and use the comprehension strategies to make meaning.

As a literacy coach and a literacy consultant we have been blessed with the opportunity to work alongside many teachers who work tirelessly to provide the best instruction they know. We diligently modeled reading strategies that Keene and Zimmerman had identified for us; we used the tangible lessons and activities with students that were detailed by Harvey and Goudvis; and we made sure to provide ample opportunities for practice. Our conferences were timely and focused and we could see that our students were becoming skilful readers. This brought a sense of pride and joy to daily interactions with our colleagues and students. Our pedagogy and practice was elevated to a new standard, and our students grew and developed as strategic readers. We are forever indebted to these literacy leaders for changing our beliefs and practice. And our students have reaped the benefits.

Just as we were becoming comfortable in explicitly teaching reading strategies, a new reader seemed to emerge in our classrooms—the skilful reader who chooses not to read. We were not alone in witnessing this phenomenon, as other literacy teachers were also beginning to see skilful readers sadly lacking the will to read. These students do not see value in reading, nor do they enjoy reading as a pastime. As a result of identifying these self-identified non-readers, reading teachers and researchers began to consider readers' interests, attitudes, and motivation as part of what it means to be a true reader. It became apparent that, along with teaching the skills, we needed to address and invest in developing the will to read. After all, what good are the skills if you do not have the will?

We longed for our students to see reading as a rewarding experience, to enjoy reading as a pastime, to choose to read in their spare time, and to carry an enthusiasm for reading beyond the classroom. We knew these to be admirable and worthwhile aspirations. What teacher doesn't dream for this to happen for students? However, we were acutely aware that there were obstacles we would have to contend with in our quest to turn students on to reading. For example, some students enter our classrooms with a sour taste in their mouth from reading the wrong things or having unsuccessful reading experiences in the past. Others have little time left for reading pursuits in their jam-packed schedules; some are glued to their phones and consider their devices another appendage. But we were willing to jump, leap, and tear down these obstacles in our mission to create wilful readers. Transferring and turning reading ambitions into reality means our explicit instruction must directly address these goals. Strategy instruction is simply not enough to ignite reading passion. As teachers, we have the responsibility, the obligation, and the duty to create an environment where kids flourish into readers who have the skill and the will.

In this book we offer classroom-based solutions that have been developed, tested, and refined over a number of years in many classrooms. It is built around six essential steps:

1. Sharing Your Reading Life
2. Knowing Your Students
3. Modeling the Habits of a Reader
4. Making the *Why* of Reading Visible
5. Creating the Space
6. Nourishing the Will to Read

With it, you can take reading instruction beyond teaching the skills to addressing the will.

In *Cultivating Readers* you will discover how to foster reading engagement through an active reading community. You will be compelled to reflect on the way in which you currently teach the will of reading, and be inspired and motivated to incorporate new ideas and strategies into your practice—to do what you do even better, just as we have!

1

Growing the Will to Read

> *A garden requires patient labor and attention. Plants do not grow merely to satisfy ambitions or to fulfill good intentions. They thrive because someone expended effort on them.*
>
> — Liberty Hyde Bailey, *Country Life in America* (1903)

Tomatoes, onions, beets, carrots, cucumbers, peppers, radishes, lettuce, spinach—the bounty that bursts forth from Jim's garden is endless. Anne's dad is known throughout the community for sharing the fruits of his labor with everyone and anyone. It's a common occurrence for neighbors to open their front door and find bags of fresh produce waiting on their doorstep. So many reap the benefits and rewards of his hard work and the endless hours he spends in the garden cultivating his crop. Unless you're a gardener, you may not realize all the time, energy, and effort that goes into a bountiful harvest. But Jim knows. It all begins with the soil that has to be turned, toiled, and tended before the first seed is dropped into the ground. Then comes the fertilizing of the soil, followed by the strategic planting of particular vegetables. Then the farmer tirelessly waters and weeds each and every day while the earth and sun do their part. Once the first sprouts appear, Anne's mother knows just where to find Jim—out in his garden coaxing and nurturing his plants to grow and flourish.

We have to admit that we do not have green thumbs. But, as teachers, we have many traits in common with avid gardeners like Jim. Teachers are dedicated, hardworking, persistent, intentional, and thoughtful—just like a gardener. But our crop is made up of students who have the skill and will to read.

The goal of the gardener is to coax and nurture his or her plants into producing a plentiful harvest. To meet this goal, every gardener has a deep understanding of what every crop needs. Student need is at the root of all we do, and it probably is for you too. As teachers we have the ability to observe situations with a keen eye and a discerning ear. We are able to dig through all the noise and activity to discover the essential learning taking place, while also recognizing the gaps and areas of need. When we examined our classroom through the lens of reading, our observations indicated that most students were able to

- accurately read grade-level text
- read with expression and intonation
- read text fluently
- talk about their reading
- identify comprehension strategies they were using to help them make meaning

We were pleased to see students who were capable, skilful readers. It was abundantly clear that our strategy instruction had met its mark. Strike up the band, let's celebrate! Getting those results took a lot of work—kudos to us and our kids. Our students could read accurately and fluently, and could make meaning from text.

However, before the reading party got started we were dismayed to discover students who

- were not excited to read (*"Ugh! Can we read for only 10 minutes today?"*)
- didn't talk passionately about the text they were reading (*"It's an okay book."*)
- were not aware of their reading preferences (i.e., genres or authors) *("I don't know what I like to read. I don't really have a favorite author."*)
- rarely shared what they were reading with their friends (*Asking the class if anyone had a great read to share resulted in blank stares and the sound of crickets.*)
- often chose books that were not age-appropriate or thought-provoking (*Students randomly selected text at the last minute of book exchange.*)
- unaware of the rewards and value of reading (*"I read because my teacher and parents make me."*)

It was clear that many of our capable, proficient readers were the farthest thing from passionate readers—their will to read was lacklustre or even nonexistent. They didn't seem excited about reading. They didn't derive joy from independent reading. They weren't actively on the lookout for their next read. They were simply going through the motions to make us happy. Think about your own classroom—does any of this sound familiar?

We compared notes about our classes with friends and colleagues and began to arrive at a description of a new reading entity. Like Lewis and Clark, we entered uncharted territory, but instead of a wilderness what we discovered was a skilful reader with no will. This new reader is proficient but disengaged. When we started to investigate this reading phenomenon, we found we were in good company. Layne, Miller, and Kittle had all seen the same reader. This reader seemed to live in Texas, Illinois, and New Hampshire, and had evidently also crossed the border into Canada! We wondered if these readers really were a new phenomenon. Had they been lurking in our classrooms for some time, but avoided detection because we had been lulled into contentment by their reading ability? We naively had thought that skill and will automatically went together, that if we taught the skills, the will to read would take care of itself! Apparently not.

Unfortunately, readers without the will to read represent a pervasive issue experienced by many teachers in our system. Ontario's Education Quality and Accountability Office statistics show that reading achievement rates in Grades 3 and 6 have increased steadily over the last number of years. As part of this standardized testing, students in Grade 3 and 6 are also asked to complete a reading survey. In particular they are asked to respond to the following prompt: *I like to read...* In the 2015–16 school year, 47% of Grade 3 students and 48% of Grade 6 students indicated they like to read "most of the time," whereas just as many Grade 3 and 6 students indicated they like to read "sometimes." This is part of a ten-year trend that shows a steady decline in students' attitude toward reading in the province.

These statistics become even more alarming when you consider the body of research on the lifelong benefits of a positive attitude toward reading:

> Students with a more positive attitude toward reading tend to be more successful in all subjects. They are more likely to read more and to seek deeper knowledge and consequently develop deeper conceptual understandings of the subject matter... (People for Education, 2011).

This is reinforced by PISA's findings that students' enjoyment of reading is one of the most important individual characteristics predicting higher achievement. As teachers, we know this to be true: students who read more develop a more extensive vocabulary, are constantly adding and building onto their background knowledge, are able to navigate text with confidence and ease. "Research also shows that 'engaged' readers are also more likely to be socially and civically engaged as well" (People for Education, 2011). There's no denying it—cultivating a reading life has long-term benefits. Even though provincial, board, and classroom data indicate that reading achievement has steadily increased, the same cannot be said for reading engagement.

Underlying Causes for the Lack of Reading Will

Countless cups of tea and several glasses of wine led us to identify our top three obstacles to creating an engaged reader.

Too Many Activities

You name it, you can do it. And most kids do! We sat down and listed the activities students are committed to in just one of our classrooms. Check out this grocery list: speed skating, dryland training, hockey, ringette, soccer, diving, tae kwon do, karate, dance, gymnastics, volleyball, basketball, piano, guitar, violin, voice, Guides, cooking class, youth group, art lessons, yoga, and cultural language classes. Gone are the days when children went outside to play after supper until the streetlights came on, as are the days when children picked one summer and one winter activity and maybe learned to play a musical instrument on the side. It is as if parents feel they are doing a disservice to their kids if they don't enlist them in everything. In striving to create a well-rounded child, we inadvertently overschedule our children to the point where there is little time left for reading. Reading becomes an afterthought at the end of the busy day, squeezed in the last ten minutes before lights-out.

Too Much Technology

Think about it: Instagram, SnapChat, Facebook, Twitter, Pinterest, Tumblr, etc. And that's just social media. Add to the mix game systems: Xbox, PlayStation,

Nintendo, Wii. And TV: cable, satellite, Netflix, Shomi, Amazon, and more all the time. All can be consumed in the palm of our hand on our phone, tablet, laptop, or on the large-screen TV. And it's not just at home: there's the DVD player in the car on the way to the grocery store and the screens at the gas station, emergency room, doctor and dentist's office. There is no escaping technology.

> *Mary*
>
> I remember being completely satisfied with the 13 channels we got on our 24-inch black and white TV.
>
> *Anne*
>
> I remember when I was the human remote control, getting up to reposition the TV aerial just to eliminate the snow from the screen of the one TV in the house.

No longer are cartoons sequestered to Saturday mornings between 7 and 11 o'clock. Children now have access to media 24 hours a day—and there are more than cartoons to see. For students inundated with other activities, screens can provide a welcome opportunity to sit and veg. They coax, entrap, and seduce them into wasting precious time that they could spend lost in an interesting book! As John Irving says, "Wherever the TV glows, there sits someone who isn't reading" (Irving, 1998).

Too Many Expectations

In our province, the Ministry of Education outlines overall and specific expectations for each subject area. There is a document each for Mathematics, Language, Science, Social Studies, Music, Drama, Dance, Visual Arts, Physical Education, and Health, and Grades 4–8 have French as well. Because the curriculum is so immense, teachers strive to make sure every moment counts and that their instruction is directly linked to curriculum. In Language alone, there are 75 specific expectations. Of the 18 that specifically target reading, none—zip, zero, zilch—address student interest and motivation to read, or explore the benefits and value of reading. Every single one focuses on students acquiring the skills.

Upon reflection, we realized that in our quest to create the skilful, proficient reader outlined in the curriculum expectations, we had completely failed to nurture the will to read. We left it out. When we looked back on our instruction, we could not find any evidence that we explicitly explored the will to read. We had clearly taught the skills. There was irrefutable evidence of that. But without a positive attitude and the motivation to use those skills, what good are they?

A Call to Action

Had we contributed to the aliteracy trend that Steven Layne so powerfully and eloquently speaks of? Because we now know there are two sides to that coin: being a complete reader involves both skill (phonetics, fluency, comprehension, semantics, syntax) and will (interest, attitude, motivation, engagement) (Layne, 2009).

In *Igniting a Passion for Reading*, Layne challenges us to create spaces where students develop a love of reading and recognize the value and importance of reading in their life. This plea is echoed by literacy leaders, including Kelly Gallagher, Penny Kittle, and Donalyn Miller, who inspire us to think deeply and critically about the importance of turning students on to reading. Surrounded by experts who have inspired us, we reflected on our current practice. While we were pondering how to develop the will to read in our students, the following questions emerged:

- How do I develop a reading community among my students?
- How do I create a classroom environment where children feel accepted and comfortable taking on the risks and challenges required to develop as a reader?
- How can I ignite a desire to read in a way that prepares students to enter the classroom with enthusiasm and purpose?
- How can I share my passion for reading with my students? (If you do not identify as a passionate reader, what impact will that have on developing your community? How can you potentially light your reading spark?)
- How might I share my reading life with the class in a way that will turn them on to reading? (If I do not see myself as an active reader, how can I begin cultivating a reading life?)
- In what ways can my students embrace reading outside of school?

In our relentless pursuit of answers, we embarked on a quest to find solutions for our students, ourselves, and our colleagues. These solutions have become our core beliefs for developing and fostering the will to read in students. We believe students must

- See reading as fun and enjoyable
- Understand that everyone grows and changes over time as a reader
- Realize that becoming a better reader takes time, effort, and energy
- See themselves as valuable members of our reading community
- Realize that we read for different purposes
- Understand that there is a world of text out there
- Know that authors matter and have something to say to us
- Uncover the vast number of reasons we read
- Value the connections with books and with one another we make as readers
- Discover their own reading habits
- Know that their teacher is a passionate, dynamic, enthusiastic reader
- Know that one of the defining characteristics of our classroom is that we are readers

Just as Debbie Miller tells us:

> Once we know who we are and what we're about in the classroom, we become intentional in our teaching; we do what we do on purpose, with good reason. Intentional teachers are thoughtful, reflective people who are conscious of the decisions they make and the actions they take; they live and teach by the principles and practices they value and believe in. (Miller, 2007, p. 4)

Driven by these intentions, we embarked on a quest to translate what we believed to be true into explicit classroom practice.

Six Essential Steps

Cultivating Readers offers you our best thinking and practical suggestions that you can choose from as you foster the will to read in your students. We are not offering step-by-step lessons, but rather opportunities for you to create your own personalized community for the students in your class or, as our friend Annette Gilbert would say, "the bums in seats." We believe it's critical that your own voice come out loud and proud. For this reason you will not find scripted lessons here. What you will find are activities that honor what we believe to be the essential steps in creating a community that cares about reading:

1. **Sharing Your Reading Life**
2. **Knowing Your Students**
3. **Modeling the Habits of a Reader**
4. **Making the *Why* of Reading Visible**
5. **Creating the Space**
6. **Nourishing the Will to Read**

These steps form the basis of the following chapters, where you will discover how we intentionally develop the will to read. We share classroom-based solutions we have developed, tested, and refined that have significantly changed the reading culture in our classrooms. We offer you tangible ways to foster reading engagement through developing an active reading community. By targeting your instruction, you will begin to build a foundation for readers who are motivated to read and will support each other on their reading journeys. For us, the rewards have been transformative. There is absolutely no going back. Our hope is that you will be motivated to adopt the belief that influencing will is as important as teaching skill. We are excited to share our best thinking with you. Let's go!

2

First Step: Sharing Your Reading Life

Get Started

The first days of school are filled to the brim with getting-to-know-you activities: Name Game, Two Truths and a Lie, Which Tribe Are You?, Classroom Scavenger Hunt, etc. These games, strategies, and activities are fun; they foster communication, cooperation, and collaboration. They are life-savers in those initial days when we are establishing community and developing routines, not an easy feat when our students are still dreaming of swimming pools, video games, and hanging out with friends. Somehow, through these worthwhile activities we get to know our students and they get to know each other—their likes/dislikes, interests, and experiences. But how well do they get to know you, the teacher? The first weeks provide optimal opportunities to nurture the student–teacher bond as well. Our students need to make connections with us and learn tidbits about our lives. It is important that we participate in the getting-to-know-you activities and share things about ourselves: that we think chocolate should be a food group; that the day can't begin before we have a cup of coffee; and that we think pets are family members. These connections build relationships fundamental to developing a classroom community.

If our goal is to build a vibrant reading community as well, then at the beginning of the school year we must create specific experiences and events that will allow that to occur. We must establish during the early days that one of the foundational blocks of our classroom community is that we are readers. A vibrant reading community will not automatically emerge merely because we are in a language arts classroom. It will not just magically happen. We cannot wish it into being. It's not as simple as providing books and time to read (not that those are not essential components of a reading community). A reading community will develop and grow only if we carve out the precious time to make it happen and put forth the effort and energy into making it come to fruition.

One way to build a vibrant reading community is to share your own reading life. Gambrell states that a key factor in motivating students to read is "a teacher who values reading and is enthusiastic about sharing a love of reading with students" (Gambrell, 1996). If we intentionally plan and devote time to this worthwhile endeavor, students will quickly discover that their teacher not only teaches reading, but also is a passionate lover of reading. They see it on the walls. They hear it from our mouths. And they feel it from the energy we mindfully put into the room. This may not sound very earth-shattering or mind-blowing, but it has to be said: kids have to know that you are a reader! In *The Book Whisperer*, Donalyn Miller cites numerous studies that highlight the importance of the teacher being a keen reader. She laments the number of preservice teachers who report being unenthusiastic about reading. How can teachers incite enthusiasm for an activity they themselves don't enjoy?

I am a Reader Who...

Anne

I am a reader who never goes to a doctor or dentist appointment without a book in my hand. I am a reader who views family dinners on Sunday as the perfect occasion to "sell" books to my nieces.

Mary

I am a reader who sees long car trips as opportunities to get lost in a book.

How would you describe yourself as a reader? Are you a reader who can spend hours wandering throughout a book store searching for your next read? Are you a reader who shamelessly makes recommendations to complete strangers? Are you a reader who gets your Amazon order shipped to school rather than home to avoid the judgment of your partner? Are you a reader who keeps a towering stack of books beside your bed to be read? Are you a reader who will forfeit a good night's sleep for the sake of one more chapter, which inevitably becomes another and another? If you answered yes to any of these questions, you are in good company.

Or are you a reader who believes you don't have time for pleasure reading? Are you a reader who finds it challenging to find text you are interested in? Are you a reader who doesn't enjoy reading as a pastime? Are you a reader who has never been inspired or turned on to reading?

Or are you somewhere in between these descriptions? No matter how you describe yourself as a reader, the fact remains that you are a reading teacher, and we believe that requires certain things of you.

Say you are looking into possible vacation destinations. You want to go somewhere exotic where you can immerse myself in local culture and get off the beaten path. After you visit various local travel agencies, it becomes abundantly apparent that one travel agent stands out from the rest: she is a true traveler. Her passion for travel, her knowledge of different companies and tours, the authenticity with which she speaks about the culture and climate of vacation destinations, and her ability to make thoughtful recommendations inspire confidence. It won't be long until you book and set out on your adventure.

So what does that have to do with reading? Everything! You are the reading agent in your classroom. You are directly responsible for creating the reading culture and climate in your room. We believe your students deserve an agent who is knowledgeable about genres, books, and authors. They are worthy of an agent who incites enthusiasm and passion for reading. Your students are entitled to a teacher who makes insightful text recommendations and sells them on books. We cannot say it any other way. You have to be a reader!

Foster Your Own Reading Life

If you find yourself reading this and do not identify yourself as a reader, know that by acknowledging that fact you have taken the first step. We promise this change will not require an exercise regimen. No hours sweating in the gym. No trainer requesting, "Just one more!" No physical pain required. (Pardon the analogy if you are a workout junkie. We really do admire those of you who find a workout exhilarating and chase opportunities to release those endorphins. Sadly those little creatures seem to be elusive to us.) Rather, we're picturing you curled up in your favorite chair with a harmless book. That's not scary, is it?

Here are a few suggestions that we hope will jump start your new life as a reader. We hope that they inspire and motivate you to begin actively cultivating your own reading life. They are the initial steps you can take to carve out the time, the place, and the reading material you will need on your journey. The case is closed and the research is clear: before you can create a reading community, you yourself have to be a reader. Welcome to the club!

Reading Territories

Take Nancy Atwell's suggestion from her groundbreaking book *In the Middle* and examine your reading territories. For the next week grab a pencil and piece of paper (or your phone) and track all the reading you engage in. Don't censor yourself: list everything from drive-through menus and e-mails to sports scores, flyers, and your child's school newsletter. Acknowledge and honor the fact that you actually read a fair amount and you gain a tremendous amount of information from reading. We think you'll be quite surprised to discover the sheer volume of reading you do on a daily basis. Come on, it's time to celebrate the reader in you! There are no reading police out there to evaluate the quality of your reading.

> *Anne*
>
> One of the things I most look forward to when getting my hair done is the smorgasbord of magazines at my fingertips: *US Weekly*, *Closer*, *People*. If you are the same, unabashedly record them all on your list!

Precious Time

We all have endless to-do lists. Home, school, kids, family—you name it we seem to have a list for it. There are lists on the fridge, looking out at us from the bathroom mirror, stuck onto our computer monitors, on our phone screens. They are everywhere! As soon as one item comes off a list, two more magically appear on it. From groceries and cleaning, to returning books to the library and taxiing our kids, the list is never-ending. And for teachers, we would argue it is worse! The fact that our classrooms are like a second home and our students another family to take care of makes us the kings and queens of list-making. So the lists grow and grow to include endless hours of marking, lesson planning, book orders, field-trip forms, newsletters, phone calls to parents, etc. And on top of it all, teachers are *yes* people. We are notorious for taking on more because we long for the best for our students, schools, and communities.

Those long lists do get done, or at least what matters gets checked off. We believe that as you embark on developing your reading life you have to put reading near the top of the list, in red marker, in capital letters, and starred! Begin by making a commitment to read a certain length of time each day. Don't feel that if you haven't got an hour you can't invest in reading—you can start with mere minutes. Begin with the goal of reading fifteen minutes daily. After all, that is half the time it takes to watch your favorite sitcom, shorter than a period of hockey, and much less time than it takes for your weekly phone call to Great Aunt Ethel. To set yourself up for success, choose a specific time for reading. Maybe for you the best time is right before falling asleep with your pillows puffed up around you, or maybe it is while waiting for your daughter to finish dance class. If you purposefully plan your reading, it will get done, just like the laundry!

Marvel at Magazines

Do you have a green thumb and are constantly dreaming about landscaping your yard or wondering what varieties of heirloom tomatoes to plant? Then pick up the newest issue of *Country Gardens* or *Garden Design*. Magazines are always a great option when reading time is short and sparse. Whether you purchase your magazines from the local news stand or access them digitally, magazines abound. From scrapbooking, to current events, to travel, they seem to address every topic and interest a person could have. They offer the reader a variety of articles, an assortment of topics, and lots of visually stimulating pages. For some of us, an entire novel can be daunting because of the time commitment it requires, and the full pages, dense with text, can be off-putting. If this describes you, then magazines may be your first step to a reading life.

Guests of Honor

Mary
If I could, I would talk to Mother Theresa, Rosa Parks, and Canadian hero Terry Fox.

Consider the following question: *If you could sit down and have a conversation with three people, living or dead, who would you choose?* Baseball legends, historical figures, politicians, or entertainers might make your list. We encourage you to use this information as a stimulus to read. Autobiographies, biographies, and memoirs give you an in-depth look into someone else's life. Inquiring minds do want to know. It's no surprise that sales of narrative nonfiction continue to increase in a world where we are insatiably curious about the lives of others. So head off to your local book store and browse the biography and autobiography aisles. See who catches your eye and whose life intrigues you.

> *Anne*
>
> I used to work at a book store, and I remember the energy and buzz surrounding Frank McCourt's autobiography *Angela's Ashes*. People were caught up in Frankie's life of extreme poverty in pre-war Ireland and the challenges his family faced when they emigrated to the United States.

Stretch into Fiction

> *Anne*
>
> In the movies *Sense and Sensibility* and *Pride and Prejudice*, the time period, social customs, and relationships between classes and men and women intrigue me. So it's no surprise that historical romance is of one of my favorite genres to read. My mother, on the other hand, is a devoted watcher of police dramas. Her life revolves around *Murdoch Mysteries*, *Blue Bloods*, and the various *NCIS* series, plus syndicated airings of *Castle* and *Bones*. So again, it's no surprise that she loves to get lost in mystery crime novels.

Consider the last movie you saw and really enjoyed, or what type of TV shows you find yourself watching all the time. A particular genre might emerge that correlates with a specific section of books in your neighborhood library. Mystery, Science Fiction, Romance—whatever taste you discover you have in other media could become a reading preference for you. We recommend you run with it!

Build Your Reading Community

In the 1990s, a firestorm erupted when Oprah Winfrey launched her Book Club. Her selection and endorsement guaranteed that an author would be a bestseller by the next day. And you can't seem to go into a book store or a library without seeing Heather's Picks, staff picks, and librarian's picks. It's clear that readers like to talk and share. And now it's time for you to start doing it. We're not advocating that you jump into the deep end of the pool and join a book club this week; rather, we are suggesting that you dip your toe into a reading community. Begin by seeking out family, friends, and colleagues who read. Pick their brains for their all-time favorites, what they are currently reading, and/or suggestions of titles that are getting a lot of buzz. You'll be surprised how quickly your reading list will grow.

Share Your Reading Life in the Classroom

In the pages that follow you will discover mini-lessons that will support you in actively sharing your reading life with your students. These activities

- ask you to go back in time and uncover the books you treasured when you were young
- invite you to think about your own reading life as a child and as an adult
- support you as you reflect on the kind of reader you are (or are becoming)
- provide your students with the language and tools they will need to think about their own reading lives.

Summer Reading Footprint

Whether you spent your summer holidays reading at the lake, in a lounger by the pool, or on a blanket in the shade, you likely read over the summer. It could have been magazines, newspapers, novels, professional books, cookbooks,

Students will
- realize that their teacher has an active reading life outside of school
- see their teacher as a reader who reads a wide variety of texts for different purposes
- discover that their teacher belongs to a reading community

picture books, etc. One great way for students to discover that their teacher is an active reader who reads a wide variety of texts for different purposes is to share with them what you have read over the summer and why you chose to read it. A summer reading footprint will tell your students all that and more.

1. Gather a wide variety of texts you have read to show the scope of reading you did as an active reader. As well, have the title and author of each text pre-written on summer reading footprints. See page 31 for the Reading Footprint template.

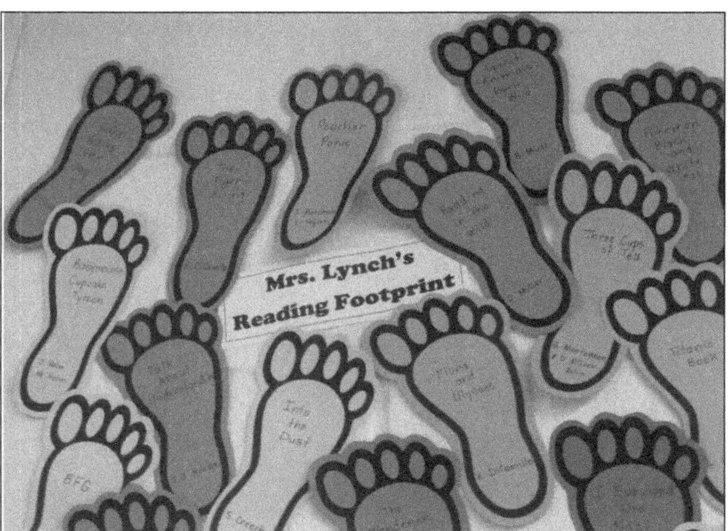

2. Use the text and the footprint to tell your summer reading anecdotes; for example:

Over the next few weeks of school we are going to get to know each other better so we can become a reading community. I am trying to get to know you and I want you to get to know me as a reader. One way to become more familiar with me is to see and hear about what I read over the summer. One of the best things I did over the holidays was go to the cottage with a group of friends. We sat for hours on the beach and passed magazines back and forth. Magazines are great for the beach because they are light reading, articles in them are short, and I don't care if they get wet! In particular I enjoyed reading this issue of In Style *magazine.*

(Share magazine)

It is filled with countless articles about the latest fashion and beauty trends. One of my favorite actresses is on the cover and I wanted to read the interview with her. I also have a group of teacher friends that I get together with regularly over the summer. We decided to read a professional teaching book so that we can become better teachers.

(Share professional text)

This summer we read Pyrotechnics on the Page *by Ralph Fletcher. I learned a lot about helping students add specific craft techniques to their writing in thoughtful ways. I'll be sharing my learning with you over this year. Lucky you!*

3. We recommend that you share five or six pieces of text and then ask your students to turn and talk about what they have learned about you as a reader. These ideas might be recorded on a chart.

Student Links

- During the first month of school, have students track their reading so that they can create their own Reading Footprints. You might choose to gather footprints from the entire class to create an eye-catching path of reading in the hallway. Not only does this celebrate your students' reading but it also shares their accomplishments with the school community.
- Another idea is to have each student create a personal fall reading display to be posted in the classroom. What makes Kaitlyn's fall reading footprint for Grade 4, below, unique is that she chose to put it on the ceiling above her desk. This quickly inspired others to want their displays put on the ceiling as well; this led to many trips to the custodian's room to retrieve the ladder. What a nice problem to have!

- You might also choose to have student reading footprints "grow" throughout the term, as shown in Celeste's display seen to the left.

Summer Reading Shelfie

Students will
- realize that their teacher has an active reading life outside of school
- see their teacher as a reader who reads a wide variety of text for different purposes

Are you caught up in the selfie craze? It seems like you can't go anywhere without seeing someone with their arm outstretched, pouting duck lips, their faces angled for the perfect shot. Despite the fact that we're all different, all selfies seem to look the same. But not our summer reading shelfies! Each shelfie, or selfie featuring the stack of books read, is unique, representing the time spent reading over the holidays.

1. Gather up a stack of texts that you read over the last weeks and that you are open to sharing with your students. Be creative but, at the same time, reasonable. It's not about building the leaning tower of Pisa out of books; it's a snapshot of your summer reading. Be open to including a variety of texts: the newspaper, adult fiction, pamphlets or a map from your holiday, a young adult novel, a picture book, perhaps even your Kindle/Kobo, and perched on top could be your recipe box.
2. Snap a selfie with your collected texts.
3. Use the photo to tell your summer reading anecdotes, sharing five or six pieces of text and then asking your students to turn and talk about what they have learned about you as a reader. These ideas might be recorded on a chart.

Anne

I posted the photo of my reading shelfie on the door to greet students on their first day. Even though I didn't plan to talk about it that day, it did create a little buzz among students.

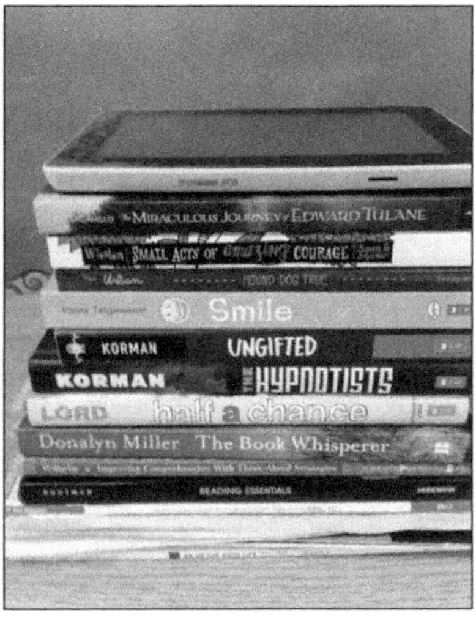

Student Links

- This activity is not one we encourage our students to replicate at the beginning of the year. Once we have invested time and energy into building our reading community, our students will be able to create an authentic shelfie that they will be proud to create and pose for.
- Taking shelfies periodically through the year can be a real celebration of the readers in our classroom. Students are delighted, as you can clearly see on their faces in the samples.

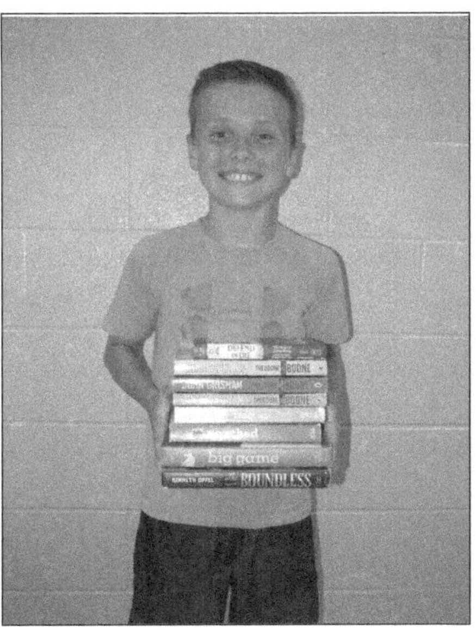

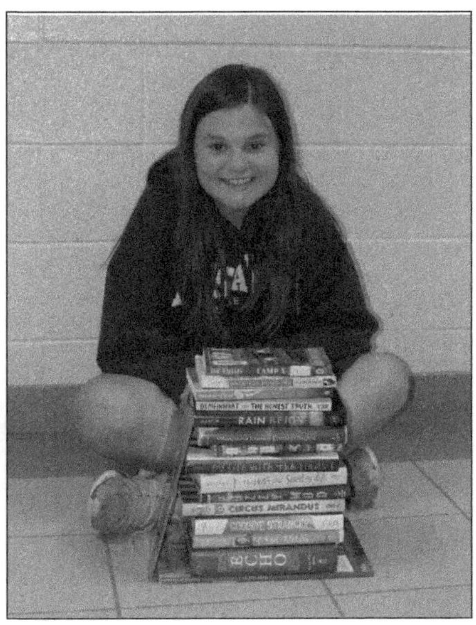

A Picture of Me

Students will
- hear and see how reading affected their teacher when he/she was their age
- discover touchstone texts that stand out in their teacher's memory
- begin to create connections with readers outside of themselves (teacher, family, friends)

Do your students think you have always been a teacher? That you sleep at the school? Are they shocked when they see you at the grocery store with your own family? I think for many of our students it is hard to envision their teachers having lives outside the walls of the school, let alone that we were ever children ourselves. One powerful way for students to realize that you were once a student just like they are is to share a picture of yourself at their age and to talk about what texts you remember reading and enjoying back then. A Picture of Me will support students in discovering the reader you were at their age and help them form a personal connection with a younger you.

1. Dust off those old photo albums and start looking for a picture of yourself when you were around the same age as your students. Mount it on poster board and ensure there is ample display space around the image.
2. Consider what you enjoyed reading as a child. Did you have a favorite book series that kept you hooked, magazines you looked forward to getting every month, a comic you read each week in the newspaper, or maybe a nonfiction text you examined countless times?
3. Look in your basement or parents' attic and find those books you loved to read. If the books were long ago donated to Goodwill, hit the Internet and search for those titles and book covers. Print a random selection (about five or six) that encompasses the variety of texts you liked to read.

Mary: My sister Kathryn affectionately remembers the *Burgess Book of Animals* that she treasured. She spent countless hours immersed in the beautiful photos and text.

Anne's Grade 6 Picture of Me shows a variety of texts:
- a popular series
- well-known authors
- a Canadian classic
- various genres

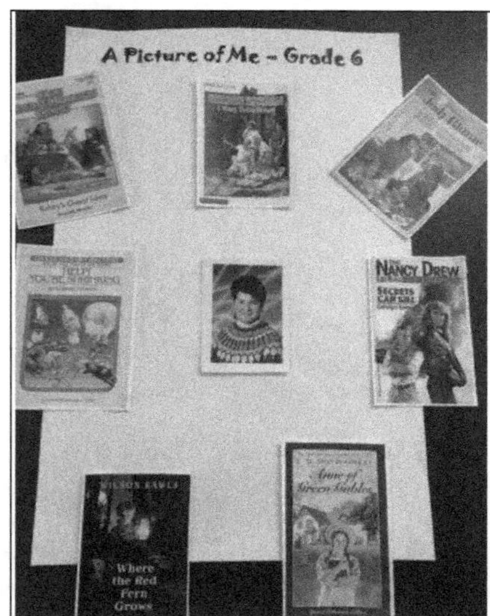

4. Students will be intrigued from the minute they enter the classroom and see a photograph proudly on display. Watch their faces as the realization settles in that it is you in the photo. Once you and your students' stop laughing at your childhood image, begin to share with them the story of your reading life at that age through the books you read. Display the book covers around your photo one at a time and offer a brief explanation of why they were significant to you:

   Do you have a favorite series you love to read? Well, I remember going to the Belmont Public Library and wandering up and down the aisles searching for my next read when I was your age. I clearly remember one day in particular when the librarian stopped and asked me a few questions. She wondered if I liked books where the main character was a girl my age and if I liked stories that were realistic. Once I answered yes to those two questions she handed me the first book in the Babysitters Club series and I was hooked. I fell in love with that unique group of friends who bonded around their common summer jobs as babysitters. I was infatuated with their lifestyle in a city that was different from my life on the farm. As babysitters, they seemed so mature and responsible, and before long that was the only summer job I wanted!

Student Links

- Have students think about the readers they are right now. Encourage them to share titles and authors that are important to them and explain why.
- Another great link between home and school is to have students talk with their parents about their childhood reads. This will help foster your growing reading community.

> *Anne*
>
> A reluctant reader in my class discovered that *Charlotte's Web* was a book that her mom remembered fondly and had cherished as a young reader. Emma arrived at school eager to locate the book in our classroom library and was determined to read it herself. Despite the fact that it was below her reading and grade level, this text proved to be a gateway title for Emma. A reading bond was established between Emma and her mother as they talked about Wilbur and Charlotte. I nurtured this budding connection between them as readers by providing them each with a copy of *The One and Only Ivan*, followed by *The Miraculous Journey of Edward Tulane* to enjoy together. A reading path was set for Emma and she has not looked back since.

- Take a picture of each student. Over the course of the school year, have students track significant texts that affected them as readers, listing the titles and authors around their photos. Consider printing the book covers so that students can create their own A Picture of Me collage. Can you imagine how powerful these artifacts could be as a reflection tool at the end of the term or school year? Not to mention the valuable recommendations they provide to nurture your reading community.

Me-as-a-Reader Timeline

Students will
- see their teacher as an active reader who has read a wide variety of text for different purposes over time
- discover that their teacher's reading life has evolved and changed over time depending on circumstances

Most days in our classrooms, students have the opportunity to see teachers as proficient readers, so we wonder if they assume that we were born this way: that we have *always* been a strong reader with an innate love of reading; that we have *always* been able to unlock print, read with fluency and expression, and comprehend what we read; that we have *always* known what our reading preferences are and selected text with ease to read and share with others.

If we don't take students back in time and share with them our journey of becoming a reader, they can be left with a lot of misconceptions. They need to be aware that every reader is on a journey, and that not every journey is skittles and rainbows. They need to see that, like them, some of us struggle to learn to read, some of us find reading a chore, and some of us would rather do anything but read. They also need to see that and that others have fond memories of cuddling with a parent and reading, have favorite authors and books they treasure. For most of us, it is a balance of both: there are times when reading is truly enjoyable and other times it is a tedious chore, depending on the text, the time in our life, and the purpose for reading.

As teachers, the reading leaders in the classroom, it is essential that we share our reading journeys with our students. We recommend displaying your reading life on a Me-as-a-Reader Timeline.

1. Print the covers of five or six texts you have read at each period of your life: preschool, elementary student, secondary student, university/college student, parent, teacher. For example, preschool years might be represented by nursery rhymes, fairy tales, books by Robert Munsch or Dr. Seuss, the Golden Book series.
2. Construct the timeline in front of your students, sharing the titles, the purpose for reading, the formats, and the memories these text experiences evoke.

Consider tackling one section of your life each day to build a sense of anticipation and excitement.

Each timeline clearly conveys that readers change and grow over time.

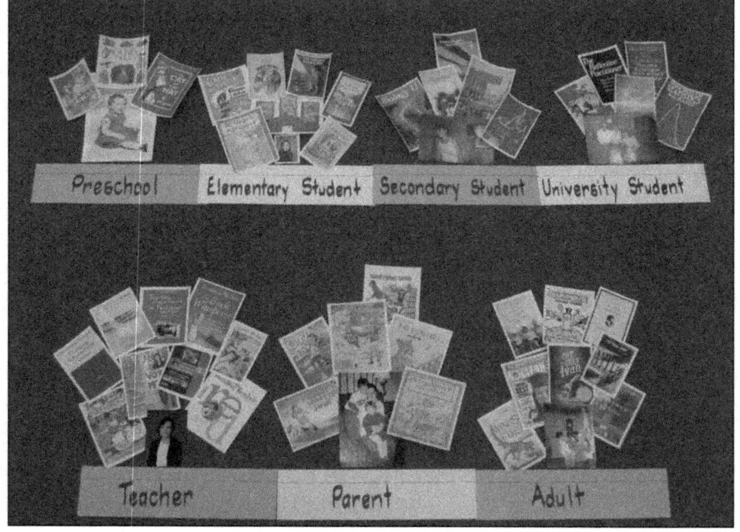

3. When sharing your Reader Timeline, it is the talk around your reading journey that is important, not the title and book summary. Talking points that may emerge from your timeline:
   - favorite authors and titles
   - choice vs. assigned reading
   - different genres and formats
   - length of texts
   - series
   - development of stamina
   - purposes for reading
   - sharing of text

Student Link

Have each student bring in a text that has been significant in their reading life. It may be a text read to them in their early childhood or one that they have read recently.

> *Mary*
>
> I remember the buzz and energy that filled the room when Marcus shared his memorable book about dragons. The fantastical illustrations and accompanying descriptions immediately caught the attention of his classmates. His willingness to share this text was appreciated as the book was passed from student to student over the next few weeks.

Daily Read-Alouds

Students will
- hear and see a proficient reader
- be immersed in quality text
- develop an awareness of the value of picture books
- bond through the shared experience of a common text

While sharing your life as a reader with your students, you need to model what a proficient reader sounds like. Each of us can remember a time when we were captivated by a story read to us. The manner in which the reader spoke drew us in; the reader's voice, level of expression, measured pace, and rhythmic phrasing mesmerized us; we were swept away and became part of the story. Sadly, read-alouds do not always work like this. We've also experienced readers unprepared to read aloud and perform for an audience.

When reading aloud, your goal is to hook listeners, draw them in, take them on a journey, and have an impact on their minds and hearts. It is a performance—and we need to view it this way. Students need to hear and see a reader who reads with great pace, tone, phrasing, expression, and intonation. Our ability to read in this manner is dependent on the quality of text we choose to share with our class. We select texts to be read aloud for a variety of purposes:
- exposure to different genres
- reading for enjoyment
- as mentor text for writing
- for making thinking visible
- as opportunities for dialogue and discussion about rich text and topics
- as fuel for higher-order thinking questions

Not just any book is going to do this or have this effect. We believe that exposing and immersing our students in quality text is fundamental. The text needs to be intellectually demanding, promote sustained classroom conversation, and be rich enough to provide a big idea that connects the reader to the world (Luke, 2014).

> Sharing things with kids that delight us, makes our eyes light up and our brains cackle and our hearts grow bigger, should be the learning target every day. Don't dumb it down... make it into the miraculous event it is, every time. Every single time you find a book that moves you, it is a tiny miracle. —Samantha Bennett (in Kittle, 2011)

Those are the texts you need to select and share.

Mindfully select different themes you want to tackle through books. For example, we have chosen the importance of libraries, the power of reading, the essential elements of community, and the value of humor in our lives. We wholeheartedly agree with Katherine Paterson:

> Give them something that is WORTH reading—something that will stretch their imaginations—something that will help them make sense of their own lives, and encourage them to reach out to people whose lives are quite different from their own. (Paterson, 1995)

The quality texts we expose our students to and immerse them in at the beginning of the year are predominately picture books. This comes as a surprise to our Junior and Intermediate students, many of whom have the impression that picture books are no longer age-appropriate for them and hold no value. They couldn't be more wrong! These books are the perfect appetizer to reading:

- Their length allows teachers to peruse an assortment to find the best fit for our readers and purpose.
- Their length means that they don't take a tremendous time commitment to read.
- They pack a punch in few pages and can tackle mature and challenging topics in accessible ways.
- The incredible illustrations appeal to the aesthetic in each of us.

Reading a text together, the whole class has a shared reading experience that bonds our community. These stories and characters become a common language for all readers in our classroom.

Let's Hear it for Libraries

Selecting text that examine libraries in many societies sends a clear message to students that we value the role of libraries in our civilized world. These buildings serve as places to unite, equalize, and spread knowledge to the masses. We have found that some students take for granted the existence of libraries in their school and community. Sharing stories where the very structure and contents of libraries are threatened are eye-opening to our students. Given the relatively quick access to books our students enjoy, many are also shocked to discover the lengths brave individuals will go to provide reading material to remote locations where books are a rare commodity. Recommended books include the following:

William Joyce, *The Fantastic Flying Books of Mr. Morris Lessmore*
Seth Roth & Karen Leggett Abouraya, *Hands Around the Library*
Margaret Ruurs, *My Librarian is a Camel: How Books are Brought to Children Around the World*
Jeanette Winter, *Biblioburro*
Jeanette Winter, *The Librarian of Basra*

Rewarding Reading

In the early days with a class, we also target books that honor reading. We want to publicly acknowledge the different journeys readers take through a reading life. Some of us have learning difficulties, others don't find reading enjoyable, and then there are those who seem to have been born with the ability and love of reading. By hearing about the reading adventures of others, students form meaningful connections with characters with whom they can identify. It sends a clear message: "It's okay to not be a reader yet, but through the conversations these stories promote I want it to be abundantly clear that everyone will become a reader in this room." Recommended books include the following:

Barbara Bottner, *Miss Brooks Loves Books and I Don't*
Oliver Jeffers, *The Incredible Book Eating Boy*
George Ella Lyon, *Book*
Manjusha Pawagi & Leanne Franson, *The Girl Who Hated Books*
Patricia Polacco, *Thank You, Mr. Falker*

Community Matters

In *The Inside Guide to the Reading–Writing Classroom, Grades 3–6: Strategies for Extraordinary Teaching,* Leslie Blauman offers a detailed lesson which we have used year after year to assist us in developing the norms for our community.

Another theme that we explore is community. The essential components of a community are responsible and respectful behavior, honoring the rights of ourselves and others, and, above all, treating each and every one with kindness (see Blauman, 2011). Recommended books include the following:

Leo Leoni, *Swimmy*
Trudy Ludwig, *The Invisible Boy*
Patricia Polacco, *The Junkyard Wonders*
Amy Rosenthal, *The OK Book*
Jacqueline Woodson, *Each Kindness*

It's Time to Laugh

According to author and renowned speaker Chuck Gallozzi,

> Laughter dissolves tension, stress, anxiety, irritation, anger, grief, and depression... after a hearty bout of laughter, you will experience a sense of well-being. Simply put, he who laughs, lasts. (Gallozzi, 2009)

We believe it is important to mindfully inject fun and humor into our early read-alouds. These books signal to students that one of the reasons we read is for enjoyment and that not all texts explore serious topics. There is a lighter side to reading to appreciate. Laughter is infectious, brings us together, and fills our classrooms with joy. And who doesn't want to share in the laughter? Recommended books include the following:

Rod Clements, *Grandpa's Teeth*
Drew Daywalt, *The Day the Crayons Quit*
B.G. Hennessy, *The Boy Who Cried Wolf*
Steven Layne, *My Brother Dan Is Delicious*
John Scieszka, *The True Story of the Three Little Pigs*
Bob Shea, *Unicorn Thinks He's Pretty Great*
Lane Smith, *It's a Book*
Suzanne Willams, *Library Lil*

The Teacher Is Reading...

Students will
- realize that their teacher has an active, independent reading life outside of school
- see that their teacher is able to genuinely recommend books because he/she has actually read them
- know that their teacher values the books in the classroom library

By this point we are sure we have convinced you that, as a reading teacher, you must be a reader yourself. But here's the catch: you have to read text at the level and interest of your students. It is now time to establish yourself as a fellow reader in the classroom community. You have to make your own reading public.

1. There are countless places you can go to find worthwhile titles:
   - your school library and knowledgeable, friendly librarian
   - book reviews in newspapers and teacher magazines
   - reputable blogs: e.g., nerdybookclub.wordpress.com, mrschueads.blogspot.com, thereisabookforthat.com
   - websites: e.g., www.goodreads.com, www.accessola.org)
   - award winners: e.g., Newberry, Caldecott, Coretta Scott King, Forest of Reading
2. Create a personal reading commitment that is manageable.
3. Post your current reading prominently in your classroom.

Anne: My commitment is to read two YA books a month.

Student Link

Be sure to keep your display up to date.

A public display of your own reading creates a sense of energy and buzz around a potential text for students to read, provides opportunities for conversations and dialogue, motivates kids to seek out or purchase the title, and holds you accountable to your goal. When you do this you distinguish yourself as a credible reader doing exactly what you are expecting your students to do. You can't fake this!

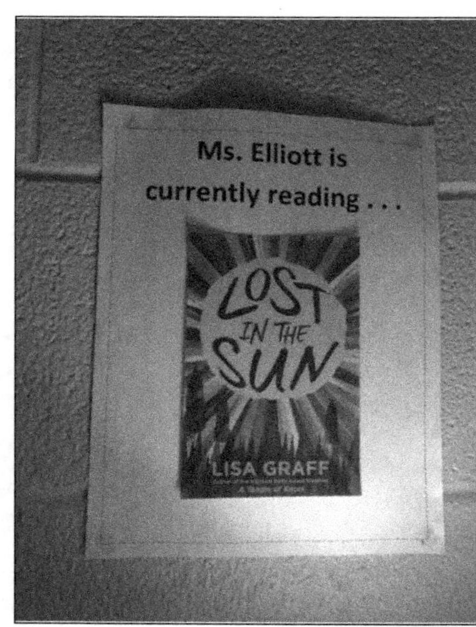

Teacher-as-a-Reader Show and Tell

> *Reader Alert: This activity will be successful and powerful only if you have engaged in the some or all of the preceding activities.*

Students will
- identify and reflect on what they have learned about their teacher as a reader from previous lessons
- summarize the key attributes of their teacher as a reader

You may not realize it but, by engaging in the activities we have outlined, you have participated in reading show and tell. Your students have had the privilege of investigating a reading artifact—you! By making your reading life public you have shown and told your students who you are as a reader in purposeful and intentional ways. Students have been shown and told the following:
- that *you* have an active reading life outside of school
- that *you* read a wide variety of text for different purposes
- that *you* belong to a reading community
- how reading affected *you* at their age
- that *your* reading life has evolved and changed over time
- that *you* are a proficient reader
- that *you* can genuinely recommend books because *you* have read them
- that *you* value the books in your classroom library

You have shown and told your students so much about you, now it's time to let the students tell you what they have learned. It is time to pick the fruit of your labors, to uncover what your students have discovered. Time to celebrate!
1. Copy and distribute the Teacher as a Reader slips from page 32.
2. Encourage students to jot down at least three things they have learned about you as a reader: e.g., *She reads with a lot of expression. He rereads books. He can only read one book at a time. His favorite series was* Anne of Green Gables. *She reads books before selling them to us. She likes to read in bed. Her favorite genre is historical fiction.*
3. Once students have had a few minutes to think for themselves and have jotted down their ideas, ask them to them travel around the room to give and receive ideas to list on their slips.

It's clear these students know their teacher as a reader.

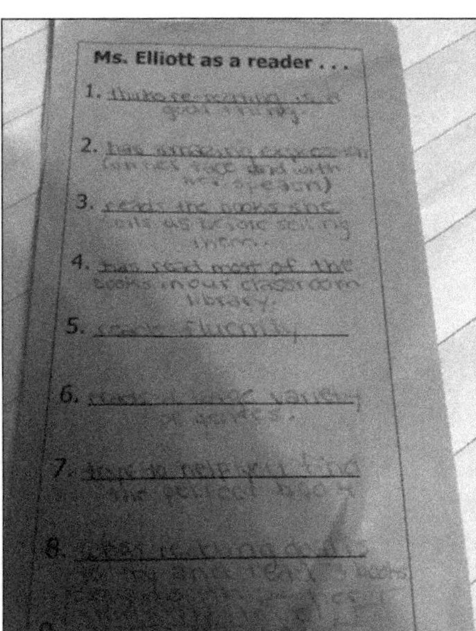

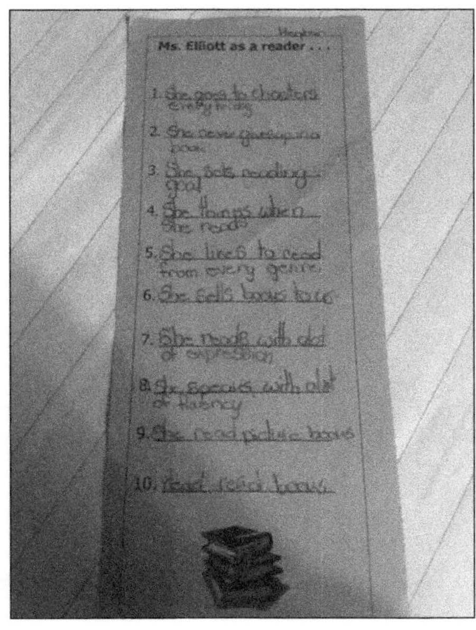

Student Links

- Use the information gleaned from students to form a chart listing the characteristics of you, their teacher, as a reader. By posting this chart in the classroom, you show that you value their thinking and learning, and you make your beliefs as a reader and your reading life public. Most importantly, you can see what your students have discovered from your sharing. This chart can grow and evolve throughout the year as students discover even more about their reading teacher.
- At Meet the Teacher Nights, it brings smiles to our faces to hear our students share tidbits of information about us with their families. It's always interesting to hear what kids choose to share from those early days: *Ms. Elliott has a golden retriever named Charlie. Mrs. Lynch has two children named Mark and Jennifer. Ms. Elliott lives on a farm. Mrs. Lynch loves going to Mackie's for French fries in the summer.* You never know what students connect with and share. It truly melts our hearts to hear students talk with authority about their teacher as a reader. Without a doubt our job is to inspire our students to become proficient, passionate readers. If we are to do that, we must share our reading lives with our students at the outset of the school year. There must be no doubt that their teacher is a reader—and they will be too!

"The reality is that you cannot inspire others to do what you are not inspired to do yourself." (Miller, 2009).

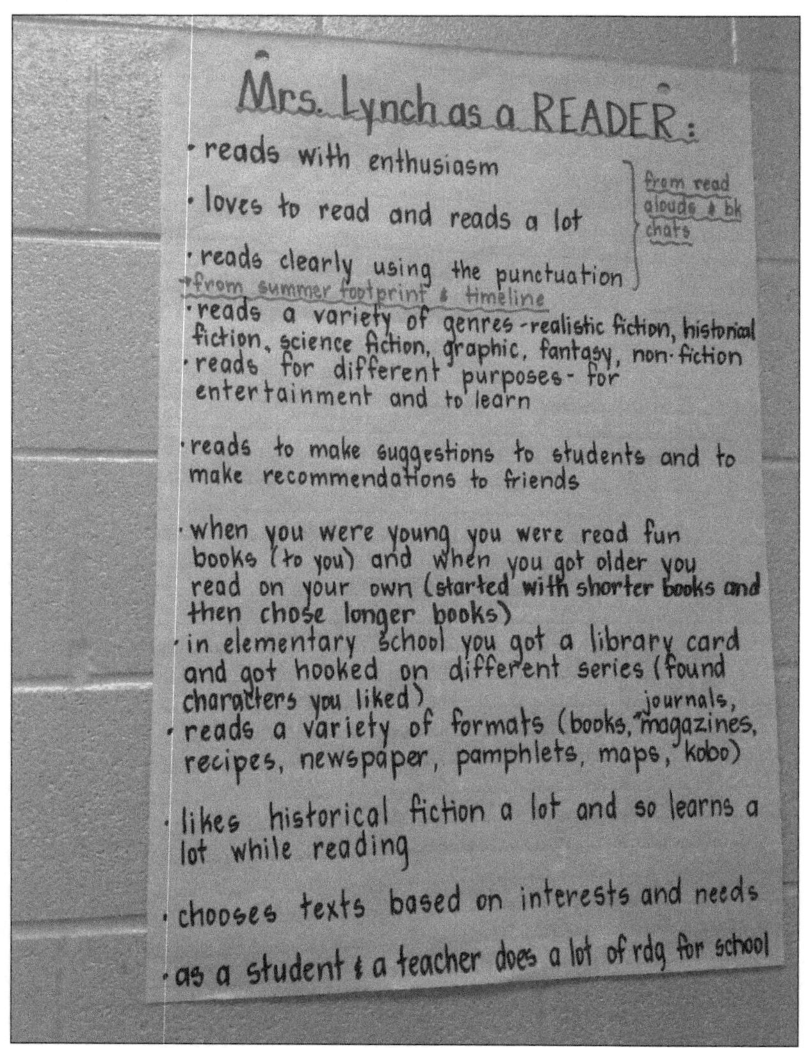

This co-constructed anchor chart reveals the characteristics of the lead reader in the classroom.

Reading Footprint Template

For each footprint, record Title, Author, and Genre.

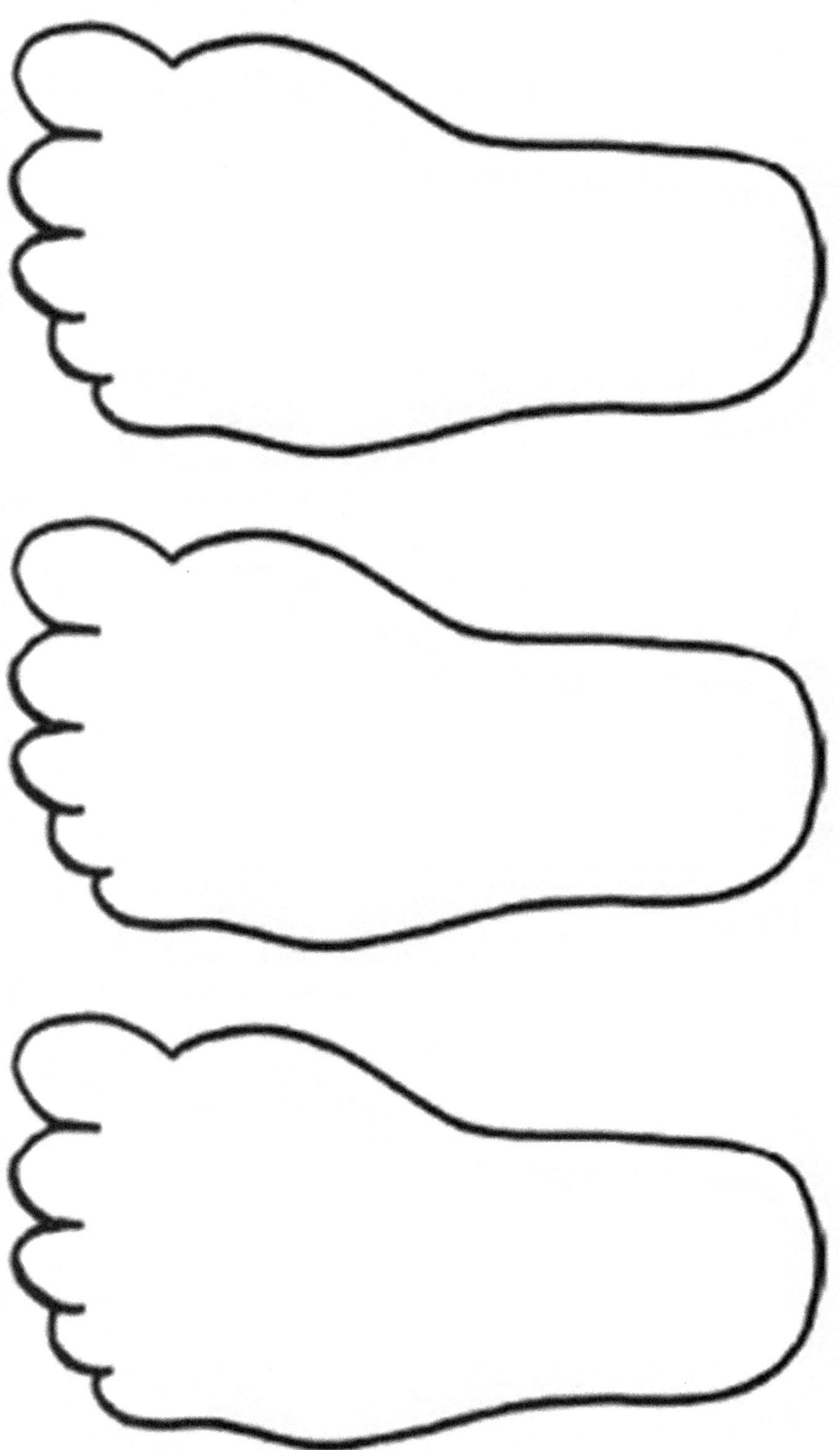

Teacher as a Reader

__________ **as a Reader . . .**

1. __________
2. __________
3. __________
4. __________
5. __________
6. __________
7. __________
8. __________
9. __________
10. __________

Name : __________

__________ **as a Reader . . .**

1. __________
2. __________
3. __________
4. __________
5. __________
6. __________
7. __________
8. __________
9. __________
10. __________

Name : __________

3

Second Step: Know Your Students

'Twas the night before school when all through the house
a teacher was stirring, as quiet as a mouse.
Her classroom was ready with books everywhere
in hope that readers would soon be there.
The teacher was nervous, on edge in her bed,
while visions of her unknown students flashed through her head.
Were they excited, anxious, or scared?
She didn't know, but she really cared.

On the night before the first day of school, teachers experience the same emotions felt by children on Christmas Eve. A sense of anticipation, excitement, and nervousness keeps them up all night. No matter if this is your first year teaching or your twenty-fifth, we all experience those first day jitters. Instead of images of the man in the red suit and visions of presents under the tree, teachers lie awake thinking of their students, wondering if the activities they have planned are appropriate, and if they have planned enough. Rather than sugarplums dancing in their heads, unanswered questions abound: *Who is the person behind each name on my class list? What are they like? Will my students gel together as a class? Will they like me? Will they go home that first day happy? Will they want to come back the second day?*

While battling these questions about a new class, we always mourn the loss of our previous students. The bonds that connected us were strong and the work we engaged in rich and deep. We remind ourselves that this took time, effort, and energy, and that once again it will take time, effort, and energy to form connections with new students and engage in meaningful work. But we long to jump into the deep end of the pool and start doing "real" work. Driven by the size of the curriculum, the immense demands we face each day, and the time constraints we work under, we want to begin our instruction immediately, to dive into the massive curriculum lying ahead of us and our students straightaway. A sense of urgency leads us to see the school year as a 100-metre sprint rather than a marathon, bursting out of the starting blocks and into the curriculum before we really even know our students. But this breakneck pace is not only counterintuitive, it also flies in the face of what we know to be good instruction.

Countless educational leaders attest to the necessity of knowing your students to best meet their social, emotional, and academic needs. If one of our foundational goals is to develop engaged readers, then it makes sense that we act intentionally to get to know our students as readers. A colleague was anxious to revamp the way in which he begins the school year with his intermediate students. He was insistent about booking a time to meet with the librarian the first couple days of school so his students could select texts. On paper, who could argue with putting a book into a child's hands those first few days? It's commendable. And if his goal was simply to ensure that each child had a book to read during independent reading time, he met his goal. But we propose that those first days of school are not merely about putting a book in every child's hands. Rather the goal is to get to know your students on a deeper level as readers, so that you can support them in their development. Teaching students how to make appropriate text selections is only one part of becoming a reader.

Reading Triage

Our students come to us with varied reading histories, as much a product of their pasts as we are. When looking at your class list before the start of school, you might have some knowledge of a few students: who was on a club or team, who has been recognized during an assembly, and who has been flagged by the previous teacher. But you probably don't know them as readers. You don't know the student who spent the summer devouring the Land of Stories series. Or the one whose family has passed around the Harry Potter books. Or which one makes regular trips to the public library. At the same time, you probably aren't aware of the students who have not read a book all summer and don't see themselves as readers. Or the student who has grown up in a reading desert.

Those first days are the perfect time to triage your class, just like a hospital emergency room does with patients. We want to create the conditions to quickly and efficiently uncover who is *developing* as a reader? Who is *reluctant*? Who is *proficient*? Whatever you call them, you need to know your student readers. Just as we intentionally invest time and energy into allowing our students to know us as a reader those early days, we need to carve out time to build the connections that will allow us to get to know them. If you've used the activities in Chapter 2, you know about co-constructing with your students a chart about their teacher as a reader (page 29). Imagine being able to construct a similar chart for each of your students over the course of the year. This is your goal. You want to know each of your students intimately as readers.

Consider knowing the following about each of your students:

- **Preferences:** genres they like to read, favorite authors, topics they enjoy investigating, series they are hooked on, formats they choose to read
- **Habits:** when they like to read, where they like to read, if they talk about their reading, if they're library users, criteria for selecting books
- **Behaviors:** appropriate pace, attending to punctuation, expressiveness, phrasing text meaningfully, monitoring comprehension
- **Reading History:** reading life from the previous school year, reading life at home, general feelings toward reading, commitment level to reading

Having this knowledge about a student is invaluable for making instructional moves, determining next steps, forming groups, building and sustaining your classroom library, informing assessment and evaluation, and communicating strengths and needs with parents.

Interest Inventory

Students will
- reflect on their preferences, interests, and hobbies

Teacher will
- begin to craft a reader profile for each student based on interests and hobbies
- be able to offer text recommendations based on information shared

> *Anne*
>
> This book is a judgment-free zone, right? I am going to confess that I have participated in Speed Dating. I sat in a line of tables, heard the bell ring, and had five minutes to quickly introduce myself and answer a series of questions. *What do you enjoy doing in your free time? Do you belong to any clubs or teams? What kinds of movies do you like? Are you a fan of any professional sports? What kinds of music do you enjoy? Have you read anything good lately?*

See pages 43–44 for an Interest Survey adapted from the work of Steven Layne and Donalyn Miller.

Are you wondering what speed dating has to do with reading? Everything, we would argue. Wouldn't you like to sit down and have similar one-on-one conversations with each of your students? We suggest you consider doing the next best thing—using interest inventories. Interest inventories enable you to maximize the amount of personal information you can get about students in a minimal amount of class time. You will gain invaluable insights into the preferences and personalities of your students from just a few questions. For example: Kate is an action movie fan just like you; six students play on the same hockey team; four kids take private music lessons; one student spends many hours a week with the theatre group Original Kids. This information will allow you to make immediate connections with your students, and to see patterns and trends between the students in your class. Interest inventories are a subtle way to get students to dig into their own lives for their potential reading territories. We encourage you to create and personalize your own interest inventory to meet the needs of your grade and students. Consider fill-in-the-blank styles, checklists, ranking grids, or a series of questions.

Reader Survey

Students will
- reflect on their reading preferences, habits, reading history, and attitude

Teacher will
- begin to craft a reader profile for each student based on the information provided
- be able to offer text recommendations based on information shared

To create a complete picture of each student as a reader we must go beyond an interest inventory. Posing specific questions in a reading survey can provide you with invaluable information regarding reading preferences, habits, and the reading history of your students. These "quick and dirty" questionnaires give an immense amount of information that will support you in triaging your class as readers. They will

- enable you to get a general sense of your class's attitude toward reading
- help you make informed instructional decisions for reading mini-lessons
- serve as the basis of your initial reading conferences with students

As part of the reading triage you are performing on your students, a reading survey is the equivalent of a diagnostic assessment. So it's important to consider how you will introduce this task to students, as well as how you will administer it. Convey to students clearly that you value their thoughts, ideas, and opinions, and that you want them to be completely honest when answering questions. Take it slow and steady when completing the survey with your students, perhaps even administering it over a couple of days. Rather than just handing out the survey and asking students to complete it independently, slow down their thinking by reading and talking out each question together:

> *Question 6 is* How do you share books with your friends? *I wonder: have you ever given a book as a gift? Have you ever been reading and wanted to talk with a friend about your book? Do you trade and share books with others? Or have you never given a book to someone else before? Search your memory before you answer. And be honest—give it to me straight.*

See pages 45–46 for a reading survey adapted from the work of Donalyn Miller. Remember to personalize it to meet your specific classroom needs.

This communicates the value of the task and importance of their truthful responses. Check out the vast amount of information that can be gleaned from reader surveys:

> Student 1 indicated that he reads every week for up to 3 hours when he has nothing else to do. He named his two favorite books as Archie comics and *Go, Dog, Go*, but cannot name favorite authors. He checked off almost all the genres.
> The student who filled out this survey:
> - Is open to reading and has a positive attitude
> - A daily reader but doesn't immerse himself for long periods of time
> - Chooses to read but as a last resort
> - Doesn't plan ahead his next read
> - Has no favorite authors and yet has many favorite genres? (Does he really know genres?)
> - His two favorite books are not grade-level text (Are these books are from many years ago?)

> Student 2 stated that she read only when "forced to." Her favorite books are both series, and one is a graphic text; she stated that she doesn't like "books with too much words on a page." She checked off other activities as things that prevent her from reading more and thinks she would read more if she "stopped playing my iPod and TV."
> The student who filled out this survey:
> - Only reads when made to
> - Has a neutral attitude towards reading
> - Plans her reading by keeping books on hand
> - Isn't invested enough in reading to challenge herself
> - Is aware that screen time gets in the way of her reading

Mary finds it helpful to compile information from the Reader Surveys onto a Class Compilation chart; see page 47 for the Class Compilation template. This assists her in identifying patterns and trends among her readers.

Extension

Consider giving students the same survey at the end of the year, after all their experiences as readers in your class. What better way to document student growth and to celebrate successes!

I Am a Reader Who…

Students will

- begin to recognize their own reading characteristics, style, and preferences

Teacher will

- begin to craft a reader profile for each student based on the information provided
- be able to offer text recommendations based on information shared

By the Friday of the first week of school we are weary and can think only about take-out food and the couch. We have attempted to make the best first impression on students and families. We imagine our students also go home that first week feeling exhausted. After all, the week has been a whirlwind of activity, centred around getting to know each other better. Sharing personal information with students at the outset helps to create initial connections and a friendly tone. However, to build a reading community, we need to dig deeper through the first few weeks of school. We must begin to explore ourselves and each other as readers.

The I Am a Reader list poem will support students in recognizing that they have developed as readers over time and have personal reading habits and preferences.

1. Use question stems for classroom discussion and to support students in thinking about themselves as readers:
   - Where do you like to read?
   - When do you like to read?
   - How do you choose books?
   - Who do you like to read (authors)?
   - What do you like to read (topics/genres)?
2. Post these questions on charts around the room.
3. On each chart, model your own thinking to help students get started.
4. Students can then travel in small groups to think, talk, and graffiti their own ideas on each chart.
5. The brainstorming activity can be followed by a conversation that highlights trends, identifies connections, and notes any "aha!"s that pop off the page.

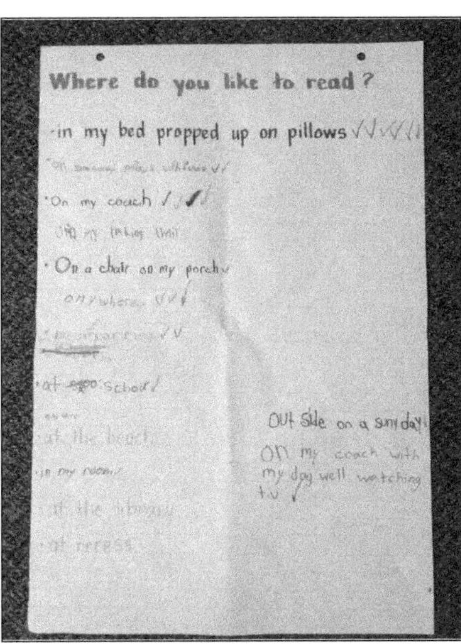

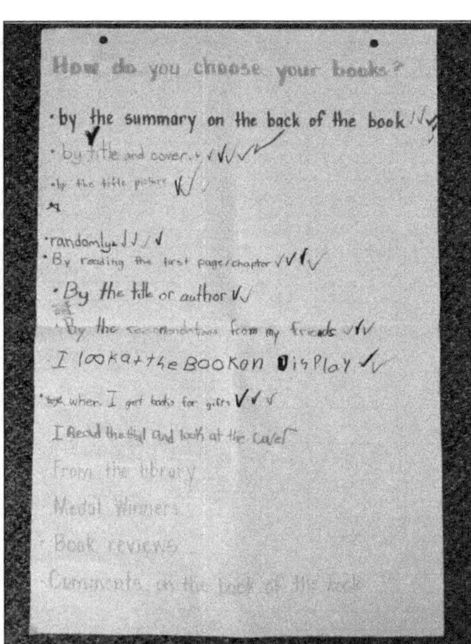

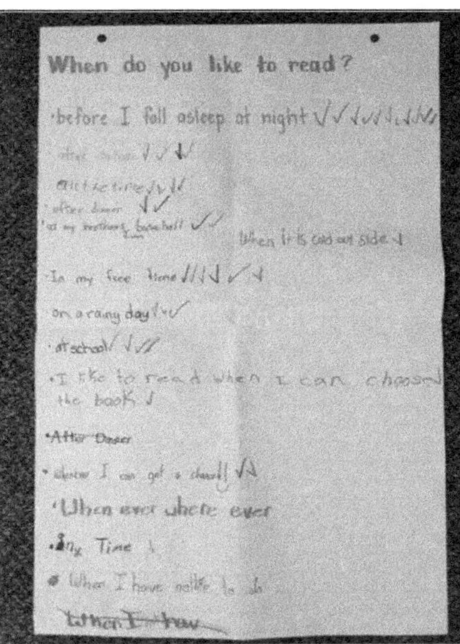

6. This information can be used by the reading community (including you) to create personal I Am a Reader list poems. Copy and distribute the I Am a Reader sheet from page 48. Ensure that student responses are varied and address a number of the question stems posed. Encourage students to

complete each sentence stem truthfully. Consider conferencing with each reader to review the completed poem and discuss the ideas shared.

> Take a look at some information these poems have uncovered about our students over the years:
>
> - I am a reader who loves to read curled up in my bed at night.
> - I am reader who needs it to be quiet with no distractions.
> - I am reader who only reads when I am told to.
> - I am reader who loves to travel back in time through books.
> - I am a reader who likes to become the main character.
> - I am a reader who likes to read about real people and real life.
> - I am a reader who has trouble finding a good book.
> - I am a reader who has a library card and goes each week.
> - I am a reader who likes to read with my Mom or Dad.
> - I am a reader who has favorite authors.
> - I am a reader who has never read a whole book.
> - I am a reader who belongs to a book club.
> - I am a reader who has trouble finding time to read.
> - I am a reader who abandons lots of books.
> - I am a reader who only likes Graphic Novels.

7. Display edited poems prominently in the class, each with an accompanying photo of the reader.

Each year we are taken aback by the honesty and transparency that our students put forth in their poems. These revelations enable us to quickly get to know our students as unique individual readers, as well as to uncover trends in our classroom.

Grade 6 sample

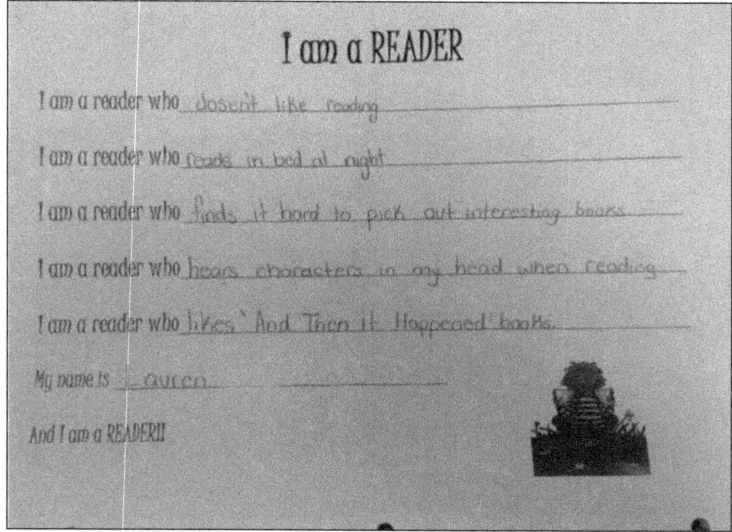

I am a READER

I am a reader who dosen't like reading

I am a reader who reads in bed at night

I am a reader who finds it hard to pick out interesting books

I am a reader who hears characters in my head when reading

I am a reader who likes 'And Then it Happened' books.

My name is _aurен

And I am a READER!!

Grade 4 sample

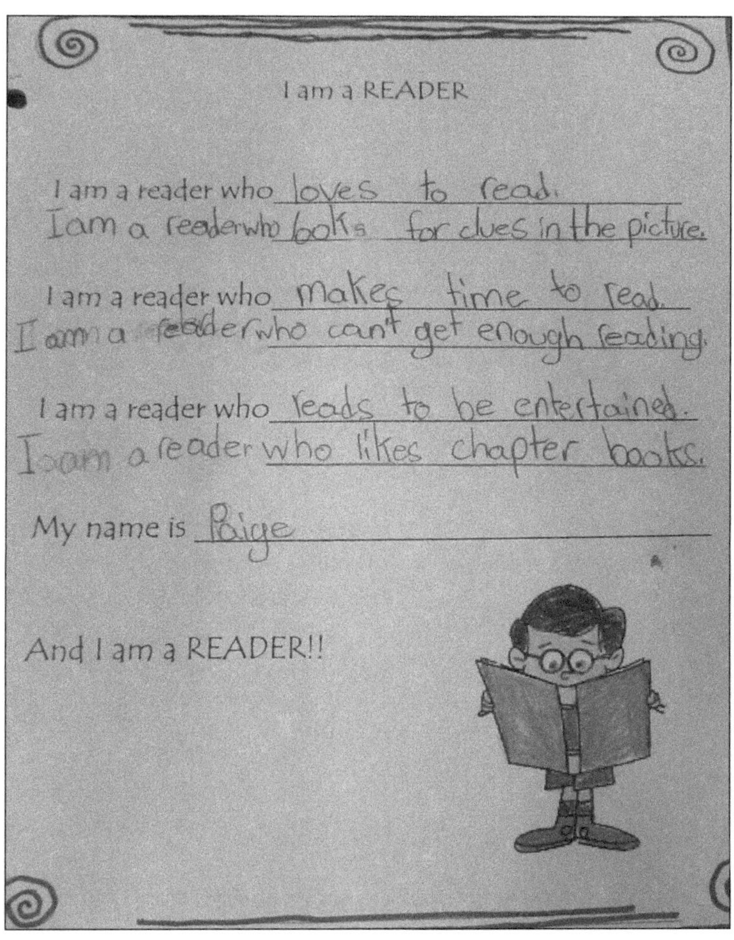
I am a READER

I am a reader who loves to read.
I am a reader who looks for clues in the picture.

I am a reader who makes time to read.
I am a reader who can't get enough reading.

I am a reader who reads to be entertained.
I am a reader who likes chapter books.

My name is Paige

And I am a READER!!

Extension

Consider having your students create I Am a Reader poems multiple times throughout the year. This activity enables students to document, track, and recognize their growth and development as readers over time. Being aware that they have improved and changed motivates students to continue on their reading journey. At the same time, it provides us with invaluable information on our students.

Home Connection

A great way to build a bridge between home and school that first month is to encourage students to have a family member write their own poems to share with the class and school. On page 49 you will find a sample letter to send home.

Students will
- reflect on their reading histories

Teacher will
- begin to get a sense of their students' reading histories
- discover genre and author trends in the class

Reader Spotlight

For the first few weeks of school you have been the star of the reading show. Now it is time to turn the tables and have your students take centre stage under the lights. Encourage students to sign up to be the Spotlight Reader for the day. Some students will be excited to have the chance to share about themselves as readers, while others may be anxious about participating because they lack a reading history. You'll know which students need a gentle push to participate and those who need to take a pass on this activity.

1. Those who choose to be Spotlight Readers are asked to come prepared with a current read, a recent favorite, and a memorable book from their childhood. Stress to students that this is a time to share why each text is significant to them, not provide a summary for each book. While each reader shares their three titles, corresponding authors, and why the texts are memorable to them, be sure to record on an anchor chart the student's thinking.
2. Once a number of students have shared, begin to mine the information for connections among the readers in the class. Kids will be excited to discover classmates who have the same interests, like their favorite authors, and/or enjoy the same series. Book buddies are born!

Extension

Over the course of the year have students take ownership for tracking and recording favorite authors and series on a chart. Make sure the charts are placed in an accessible and public place so that they can support all students in finding their next read. Or you might consider providing each student with a reading star to feature their current personal favorite on a special shelf in the classroom. Just as the local bookstore has their starred recommendations, so does your reading community.

Reading Consultation

At this point, your students have provided you with much preliminary information about themselves as readers. By completing some or all of the previous activities, you will have discovered their preferences, habits, and reading histories. This invaluable information allows you to quickly and efficiently triage your readers and diagnose them, identifying their strengths and areas of need. This enables you to consult and treat your readers in a timely, fitting, and personal manner. For example, your instructional moves become targeted to the readers in your room; your next steps are informed; your library can be revamped to meet the preferences, interests, and needs of your students; and findings will form the basis of initial conversations with students and parents.

Three-Things Reading Conference

Students will
- discover that their teacher values the personal information they have provided on their interest inventory and reading survey

Teacher will
- use the information provided by each student on their interest survey and reading survey to form the basis of their initial conference

Like first dates, first conferences can be awkward. Let's face it—you don't know each other that well, it's too early to have fully established a trusting relationship, and students feel like they are on the hot seat, since a conference is all about them! We have to be sensitive to the sad reality that some kids have never participated in a reading conference before; therefore, the idea of sitting side-by-side with their teacher can be intimidating. Without the buffer of other students, students can feel overwhelmed. It's essential that we take the lead during that first conference and put students at ease.

A strategy our mentor Charmaine Graves recommends is perusing each student's interest inventory and reading survey for three discoveries you have made about them. Using the information they have provided lets students know that you value their responses and that there was a genuine purpose to these activities.

Three Things Conference — Meghan

- plays comp. hockey, golf & tennis (very active)
- always reads b/f bed
- Fav. author: Judy Blume
- Mom recommends books
- ♡'s books with cliff hangers at the end of a chapter

Peter Sept. 10

Reader Survey

- likes to read historical texts (non-fiction)
- has trouble finding interesting fiction
- has a "negative" attitude toward rdg does not read every day

Interest Inventory

- enjoys sports, social media sites
- favourite text: And Then It Happened

We are always moved by the reaction of students when we share what we have learned about them as readers from their responses. Many are genuinely flattered, some beam with pride, others are shocked that we so closely read their surveys. Short, five-minute conferences communicate clearly to students that their teacher is paying attention, that you prepare for these visits, and that these conversations will be opportunities for instruction and assessment.

Students will

- see themselves reflected in text
- build connections and bonds between text and their own lives
- be exposed to stories and lives that are drastically different than their own lived experience

Teacher will

- intentionally select read-alouds that honor students' lives and experiences
- purposefully select read-alouds that move students beyond their own lived experiences

Windows, Mirrors, and Doors

Threading itself through all curriculum areas, reading enables us to make connections to information, to world issues, and, most importantly, to each other. It truly informs the mind and moves the heart, allowing us to live more lives than we can ever live. Reading enables us to peek through the window into someone else's life, to look into a mirror and see ourselves reflected in a story, or to open a door and enter another world. We empathize with characters and they allow us to vicariously live a life not our own. When we read, we cease to be ourselves and become the character. With Kek from *Home of the Brave* by Katherine Applegate, we struggle with feelings of loneliness, isolation, and a lack of understanding in an unfamiliar world. Reading *Each Kindness* by Jacqueline Woodson, we relate to Chloe's internal conflict about the new girl Maya and grieve the loss of opportunity for friendship. Reading *Echo* by Pam Munez-Ryan, we are swept away with the challenges Friedrich faces on his emotional journey.

When reading we also are able to travel through time and space, to explore foreign lands and experience different cultures. In *The War that Saved My Life* by Jennifer Brubaker-Bradley, we escape an abusive parent and a city at war to lead a new life on the coast of England. In *Birmingham, 1963*, we discover lives shattered by the bombing of the 16th Street Baptist Church during the civil rights movement, as the names of four little girls are imprinted on our hearts.

We firmly believe in the transformative power of reading and its ability to speak to our hearts and minds! We are readers, and our daily read-alouds communicate our belief in the power of books to be windows, mirrors, and doors to experiences beyond our own.

As our knowledge of our students increases over the first few weeks of school it is important for us to begin to track key territories to touch on during our read-alouds. For example, knowing that Monique was adopted from China, that Tarek's family emigrated from Kuwait, that five students are Indigenous and live on a reserve, that a number of students travel between two homes—all this information can and should be used to influence our text selection. Carefully search your classroom library, school library, and local library for titles that will honor these children. One person's mirror is another person's window. When your students see themselves represented in text you have chosen, you communicate to them that you see them, you know things about them and that they belong in this community.

Interest Survey

Name: ______________________

1. What do you like to do when you have free time?

2. What are your favorite TV shows?

3. Do you watch professional sports (e.g., NHL, MLB, NFL, PGA, MLS, etc.)?

4. What kind of movies do you watch?

5. What kinds of music do you listen to (favorite group/instrument/musician/musical group)?

6. What school clubs or teams do you belong to?

7. What clubs or teams do you belong to outside of school?

8. What three wishes would you like granted?

Interest Survey (cont'd)

9. If you could travel to any place in the world, where would you go?

10. If you could go to any place and time, real or imagined, where would you go?

11. If you had the chance to meet any person, living or dead, who would it be?

12. Fill in the blank: If ____________________ recommended a book to me, I would probably read it.

13. What kind of books do you own?

14. If you could pick three books to own, what would they be about?

Circle anything on the list below you would like to know more about.

crafts	history	poetry	dancing	jokes	aliens
construction	foreign lands	theatre	singers	magic	travel
electronics	printing	cars	planes	sports	health
famous people	art	animals	detectives	drawing	conservation
music	electricity	insects	outer space	writing	experiments
woodwork	monsters	science	cooking	trains	games

Adapted from Steven Layne and Donalyn Miller.

Reader Survey

Name: ____________________

Please be honest when answering these questions. I'll use what you share here get to know you as a reader.

1. If you had a choice to read every day or not, would you? ❑ Yes ❑ No
2. What time of day do you read?
3. Where do you read?
4. About how much time do you spend reading in a week?
5. Check as many as you like: *I usually read*
   - ❑ Picture Books
   - ❑ Early Chapter Books
   - ❑ Grade 4–6 Books
   - ❑ Pre-Teen Books
   - ❑ Young Adult Books
   - ❑ Adult Books
   - ❑ Other: ____________________
6. What are your two favorite books?
7. Who are your two favorite authors?
8. Check as many as you like: My favorite kinds of reading are
   - ❑ realistic fiction
   - ❑ nonfiction
   - ❑ poetry
   - ❑ fantasy
   - ❑ historical fiction
   - ❑ science fiction
   - ❑ mystery
   - ❑ humor
   - ❑ graphic text
   - ❑ biography/autobiography
   - ❑ myths, legends, folktales
   - ❑ other: ____________________
9. Do you share books with your friends? ❑ Yes ❑ No

   If yes, how do you share books?

Reader Survey (cont'd)

10. Check as many as you like: *I find books to read*

- ❑ on websites/blogs
- ❑ by having favorite authors
- ❑ by browsing bookstores
- ❑ through social networking sites
- ❑ when friends recommend them
- ❑ through book reviews
- ❑ when teachers/librarians/parents recommend them
- ❑ through book clubs
- ❑ at garage sales
- ❑ other: ____________________

11. Do you know what you will be reading next? ❑ Yes ❑ No

Check as many as you like: *I know what I'm reading next because I*

- ❑ keep a reading list
- ❑ follow new books by authors / in a series
- ❑ reserve books at library
- ❑ keep a stack of books ready to read
- ❑ finish one book, then look for another
- ❑ other: ____________________

12. Check as many as you like: *I would read more if*

- ❑ I didn't have so much homework
- ❑ I could find anything interesting
- ❑ I had more books
- ❑ my friends read
- ❑ I wasn't so busy with other activities
- ❑ other: ____________________

13. Circle the number that represents how you feel about reading.

1	2	3	4	5
YUCK!				LOVE IT!

14. How could you make more time for pleasure reading?

15. What would make you a better reader?

16. What is your reading goal this year?

17. What else do I need to know about you as a reader?

Adapted from Miller (2014)

Class Compilation: Reader Surveys

Name	Average Weekly Reading	Book Selection Practices	Preferred Text Formats	Favorite Books	Favorite Authors	Favorite Genres	Reading Attitude Rating	Reading Goal

I Am a Reader

I am a reader who ______________________________

______________________________.

I am a reader who ______________________________

______________________________.

I am a reader who ______________________________

______________________________.

I am a reader who ______________________________

______________________________.

I am a reader who ______________________________

______________________________.

My name is ______________________________

And I am a reader!!!

Pembroke Publishers ©2017 *Cultivating Readers* by Anne Elliott and Mary Lynch ISBN 978-1-55138-324-8

Family Letter: I Am a Reader

Dear Parents,

In our classroom, we are working together to build a community of readers. Today, we talked about our own reading lives and the kind of readers we are. Each student wrote a poem called "I Am a Reader" to describe himself/herself as a reader. We would like to invite you to join our community of readers by writing your own poem and sending it back to school. Below is a sample of the poem I wrote about myself:

I Am a Reader
I am a reader who keeps a stack of books to be read beside my bed.
I am a reader who recommends books to friends.
I am a reader who loves to read curled up with a blanket in bed.
I am a reader with a long, long, Amazon wish list.
My name is ____________________
And I am a reader.

Please complete your own I Am a Reader poem on the template attached.

Students have also been asked to become detectives, searching for readers in their homes. Each student is asked to find/catch a family member reading in their natural habitat, snap a photo or photos, and bring that photo to school to share.

Please return completed poems and printed photos by ________________________________. Thank you very much for supporting your child and joining our community of readers.

Sincerely,

4

Third Step: Modeling the Habits of a Reader

Anne

I really admire colleague and friend Deb Austin. She truly embodies the will to be physically active. Deb ensures that each day includes the opportunity to engage in physical fitness, whether volleyball, tennis, floor hockey, or yoga. Every day she plans which activity to participate in, what facility she is going to do it at, and when. We joke that she is always ready, willing, and able to play. Her trunk is a gym locker, full of workout clothes, running shoes, racquet, knee pads, mat, etc. Recently she met the goal of a 30-day yoga challenge! Most, if not all, conversations with her include some tidbit about her activities—the score, the endorphin rush she got, the play that won the game. Deb and I couldn't be more different when it comes to our commitment to physical fitness—I can't seem to even consistently attend my weekly walking group. But when I stop and think about it, Deb and I actually do share similar enthusiasm for our habit. But in my case it isn't physical fitness, it's reading.

We truly embody the habits of readers. We ensure that each day includes the opportunity for us to read. Whether it's the newspaper, the latest issue of our favorite magazine, an ILA article, a historical romance, or the Nerdy Book Club's newest recommendation, we read. We're never left twiddling our thumbs or forced to look at the screens in a waiting room because we always have reading materials with us. We joke that the first requirement of a purse is that it will fit at least one paperback. Even if we go an entire day without having the chance to read, we know that before we turn out the lights we will make time for our daily fix. Like Deb's 30-day yoga challenge, we meet challenges as readers too. We recently participated in the Forest of Reading nomination process and read twenty titles for students in Grades 4–8. Our passion for reading also seeps into many daily conversations. While Deb is nattering to us about skating on the lake near her cottage, we're "selling" her books to read by the fire. We're always eager to talk books, even with total strangers at Chapters, much to the embarrassment of our families.

For Deb its physical fitness, for us its reading. What is it for you? Scrapbooking, running, cooking, quilting, playing an instrument—no matter the activity, the habits are the same. We **plan:** what we're going to do, when we're going to do it, and where. We **find** all the appropriate materials we require. We **act:** we think about what we're doing, talk to others about our activity, and share our enthusiasm. We **set goals** that are realistic and manageable, and yet push us to new heights. The habits of individuals who have the desire and will to engage in a particular activity are the same!

Wilful Habits

It would be impossible to have a conversation about the habits of readers without acknowledging the ground-breaking research of Miller and Kelley. The responses to their Wild Reader Survey, completed by 800 participants, presented them and us with an operational definition of a reader through their daily habits. In their book, *Reading in the Wild*, they "identified five general characteristics that lifelong readers share" (p. xxiii):

- They dedicate time to read
- They self-select reading material
- They share books and reading with other readers
- They have reading plans
- They show preferences for genres, authors, and topics

Miller and Kelley's findings concurred with and validated our thinking around reading habits:

- Wilful readers plan. They know what they're going to read. They dedicate specific times in their day for reading, and have their favorite spaces and places at school and home.
- Wilful readers find books to read. Passionate readers are like bloodhounds in their ability to sniff out titles that hook, fit, and engage them. Being aware of preferences, they seek out their favorite genres and authors to find just-right titles.
- Enthusiastic readers act in specific ways. They think about their reading. Their excitement and enjoyment for texts is palpable. We hear it in their voices that will not be silenced.
- Dedicated readers set goals. As we support young readers in beginning their lifelong reading journey, it is important that we assist them in setting appropriate, specific, and manageable goals that fuel them as readers.

It is essential that we, as teachers, truly believe it is our responsibility to model and teach the habits that develop a passionate reader. They look straightforward: Plan, Find, Act, Set Goals. But don't be fooled by their seeming simplicity. Developing ingrained and automatic reading habits takes time, effort, and energy on behalf of the teacher in modeling these habits and on behalf of students in practicing them. We need to teach them in a manner that students will internalize and adopt.

Just as we have conveyed the importance of providing concrete and tangible learning experiences for our students, we must take the time and make the effort to teach the habits. You've heard the line, "It takes 30 days to develop a habit." As classroom teachers we have approximately 185 days to blatantly model, fully develop, and grow these habits in our students. It is not enough to merely identify the routines and tell our students to do them. Students require frequent and repeated opportunities to know, grow, and show. Subsequent lessons will help you begin to model and teach the habits of a wilful reader.

Celebrating Commitment

Students will
- begin to recognize that developing a habit requires commitment, dedication, and intentionality

As the reading leader in the classroom, it is essential that you share and model the habits of an active reader. A good way to begin is to select a person of interest for your students (e.g., an athlete, singer, dancer, or musician) and deconstruct the habits that have contributed to their skill development and success. When attempting to illustrate that developing a habit requires commitment, dedication, and intentionality, Canadian teachers often use a hockey hero as a hook. Every Saturday night, many Canadian homes are glued to the TV, watching Hockey Night in Canada. Children of all ages and genders watch their heroes take to the ice and wow us with their tremendous skill and ability. But do students realize that these athletes didn't just arrive at the arena the first time, strap on their skates, hit the ice, and excel at the game? Do they know that countless hours each and every week, on and off the ice, have been dedicated to prepare for the game? Well, let's make them aware! Let's show them!

1. Select an individual that your students know, are interested in, and admire. Remember those interest inventories—did you notice a common interest among your students? Consider that as the perfect place to search out a personality. Print a photograph of that individual and mount it in the centre of a piece of chart paper.
2. Begin by asking students to consider: How do you think this person plans for the main event (i.e., game, show, performance)? What do they do to prepare? How do they ensure they are ready? Have students brainstorm or popcorn out ideas and record them on the chart.

> *Anne*
>
> In my hockey-obsessed classroom I selected Sidney Crosby. When investigating Sid the Kid, I guided students to think about his
> - practice schedule
> - workout routine
> - diet
> - equipment
> - participation in team meetings
> - review of game footage

3. This attention on a "successful" individual is meant to elicit the intentional ways in which they **plan** what they're going to do, when they're going to do it, and where; how they **find** the appropriate materials they will require; the ways in which they **act** by thinking about what they're doing, talking to others about their activity, and sharing their enthusiasm; and the **goals they set** that are realistic, manageable, and yet push them to new heights.

Student Links

- Encourage your students to investigate a famous person to uncover the time and energy they devote to honing their skills. Their investigation should reveal the habits that contribute to that individual's success.
- You might be able to use your own classroom as the subject for this lesson. Every class has an athlete, whether it's tae kwon do, cheerleading, soccer, or dance. Celebrate a student's commitment by asking him or her direct questions to reveal how they plan, find, act, and set goals. This will not only uncover the essential habits but will also develop a sense of community.

The Habit of Planning *What*

Anne: As we write this particular chapter on the Habits of a Reader, my mind is drifting to my latest read by Linda Lael Miller. I can hardly wait to curl up in bed with Mace the cowboy winemaker from Wyoming. I bemoan the fact that I have a long to-do list that has be tackled before I can catch up with Kelly and Mace and their romance.

Readers plan. They know when, where, and what they are going to read: 10:30 p.m., bed, romance novel. Time and place are important, but it all starts with what you're going to read. Readers who are aware of their reading preferences do not find it a struggle to locate text that they are interested in and long to read. In fact, they often have to exert restraint when going to the book store. However, growing readers are on a journey of self-discovery. They are in the midst of learning what their preferences are and what books match those preferences. Texts that they enjoy often elude them, since as readers they are unsure and unaware of what their reading preferences are, and they have limited knowledge of genres, series, and authors.

The *Kids and Family Reading Report* from Scholastic indicates that "41% of kids have trouble finding books they like, especially as they get older." And that's where the teacher comes in. You are the lead reader in the classroom, the unofficial reading ambassador. It's not surprising then that "51% of kids turn to the teacher or school librarian to help them make selections" (Scholastic, 2017). It's your obligation and your privilege to support students in finding text. You need to model, teach, and support them in learning their preferences and appropriate selection techniques. This begins with developing an awareness of the immense variety of text that is out there for them to choose from.

Browsing Baskets

Students will
- select reading materials that honor their reading preferences and interests

Teacher will
- observe student reading-selection behavior
- begin to note what genres of text students gravitate toward

During the first days of school we communicate thousands of messages to students about our classroom. But one of our top priorities must be sharing the message that this is a community that reads starting on day one.

Before students begin to check out text, it's important that they browse the classroom library in a manageable way. They need an opportunity to discover the vast amount of text available to them in the room, as well as to discover the type of text valued and considered real reading. You want to send the message clearly to students that newspapers, magazines, picture books, nonfiction, graphic texts, and novels are all legitimate and respected reading material.

1. Select for each group of five or six students about twenty different titles. Make sure that each basket or bin contains a variety of text types and levels. If your classroom library lacks nonfiction text or magazines, tap into the resources available at your school or local library.
2. Turn those bountiful browsing baskets over to your students for independent reading.

3. While students are perusing their basket, keep a close eye on what's happening. You'll discover some interesting habits: e.g., Charlie consistently picks nonfiction from the baskets; Ravi flips through the books like a deck of cards; Keisha gravitates to the novels and carefully reads the blurbs on the back.
4. If a student asks to keep a title, the answer is, of course, yes. But don't communicate to the class that selecting a text from the basket is an expectation of independent reading time, because it isn't. The purpose of this activity is to expose students to the wide variety of quality reading material available to them in the classroom.
5. Over several days, rotate the baskets amongst the groups to ensure that students have sampled each basket and its contents.

Genre Sort

Students will
- understand that there are a variety of reading genres, each with its own distinct characteristics

Teacher will
- discover students' background knowledge about genres

Chapter books, novels, fiction—most students think they are one and the same. Students seem to be unaware that within the large fiction family there are a variety of distinct genres that are quite unique and different from one another. As we work to cultivate readers in our classrooms, it's imperative that we expose students to the different genres that exist to expand their reading lives. We also need to give students the vocabulary to communicate their reading preferences to others and to confidently speak the language of books. When supporting students in text selection, the starting point is usually genre, so let's make sure that students know the types and their characteristics. A genre sort will allow your students to share their background knowledge about genres as well as provide you with information.

1. Have students separate into groups of four.
2. Reproduce and cut apart a set of Genre Characteristics cards (page 76) and Genre Labels cards (page 75) for each group. Place both sets of cards in an envelope for each group.
3. Provide each group with an envelope. Ask groups to read the cards and match the appropriate label with its characteristics.
4. Pay attention to group conversations. Which genres are students able to match with ease? Which lead to debate and confusion? Are there genres they have never heard of? Be sure to consolidate student understanding and clear up any misconceptions.

Note that there is a blank card included so that a genre your class is studying can be added.

Extension

Consider having your students match a text with each genre. This activity will allow you to document and track their experience with different genres and is a way for students to share their reading lives with their classmates. It also tells you what genres students have limited experience with.

Book Buffet

Students will
- learn that, as they are growing readers, it is essential that they sample/taste a variety of genres

When you hear the word "buffet" do you see an endless spread of delectable delights, a plethora of food choices just waiting for you? When we're trying to turn kids on to reading, it's important to take them to the reading buffet, to show them the massive variety, choice, and selection of text available to them, metaphorically and physically. But before you spread out those books and allow kids to dig in, let's take the time to explain our rationale for a healthy reading diet to them.

We often start this discussion with an analogy about going to the buffet with children who eat only what they know. How sad it is to see their plates with a mountain of fries, or a few chicken balls, or only macaroni and cheese. Not only does this represent a reluctance to try something new, but it is also unhealthy. As teachers we see this in our classrooms too: students who merely read the same type of text, author, or series all the time. Don't get us wrong, we want students to have reading preferences, but as developing readers they should not be limited by those preferences. Growing healthy young readers means exposing them to a wide reading diet of mystery, fantasy, realistic fiction, historical fiction, nonfiction, poetry, etc. If you only ever eat mac and cheese, your body will lack essential nutrients, not to mention the tantalizing tastes you'll miss out on. If your reading diet is only graphic text, you will be using only particular parts of the reading brain while neglecting others. As well, imagine all the spectacular text you would miss out on simply because you refuse to read anything that is not a graphic text. Students need to understand that there is a rationale behind them being encouraged to eat/read a variety of texts.

Following this conversation, have students reflect on their reading diet and share with an elbow partner their reading preferences, as well as genres they have yet to sample and taste. Once your developing readers are aware of their reading diet, it can inform future text selection. So let's take them to the buffet and have a feast.

The Habit of Planning *When*

Now that we've explored the breadth of what students can and should be reading, it's time to turn our attention to when. Just as important as knowing what we're going to read is deciding when we're going to do it. As teachers, we have witnessed a student take home a book night after night, never seeing the bookmark move once. Or students return library books they were originally excited to read without even cracking the cover. We're not talking about a student's inability to make an appropriate text selection; rather, they did not dedicate the time to reading. Reading the book wasn't a priority. It would appear it wasn't even on their radar. We must be upfront with students that becoming a reader requires a time commitment on their part.

In *The Power of Reading* Steven Krashen concludes, from a meta-analysis of more than 50 reading research studies, that when children are given adequate time to engage with texts on a daily basis, their improvement in literacy development is substantial. He contends that Free Voluntary Reading (FVR) has a dramatic influence on students' comprehension, vocabulary knowledge, spelling, writing ability, and overall academic achievement (Miller, p. 51). From Allington, to Beers, to Routman and Atwell, through Miller, Gallagher, Kittle, and Layne—the list of literacy leaders who believe in the importance of daily reading time is long. So please add our names to that list. It's a given; it's established; its irrefutable. Kids have to read!

Students will
- begin to develop the habit of reading daily, inside and outside the classroom
- recognize that developing this habit requires a time commitment, dedication, and intentionality on their part

Let's Make a Deal

Have you ever watched the game show "Let's Make a Deal"? Selected contestants are offered the chance to make a deal, often involving a choice between two or three unknowns. It's always gut-wrenching to see contestants pass up a wonderful prize and get essentially nothing. Luckily, you get to make three deals with your students and each one is a win, win, win. As the lead reader in the room, you want to build a relationship with students as readers by promising to give them time each and every day to exercise themselves as readers. In turn, your students pledge to themselves and us that they will commit to developing the habit of reading outside of school. As well, we want to show students how to find and carve out time throughout the day for reading. Here are the three deals:

1. **Promise** in-class daily reading time
2. **Pledge** to read at home
3. **Plunder** undedicated minutes for reading time

1. The Promise of Time

The beginning of the year will look different from the end of the year, as your students build reading stamina. So be realistic in terms of how long your students can sustain independent reading at the outset of the year, especially since some students will not have engaged in this worthy activity over the summer holidays. As well, the time you allot to reading will vary depending on the grade and age of students you teach.

Let's show students how invested we are as teachers in their development as readers by providing them with no less than twenty minutes of independent reading time every day. This is an essential habit for your class to develop as a reading community. This is sacred time, non-negotiable. Assemblies, guest speakers, or field trips cannot get in the way of providing students with time to practice reading. At the outset of the school year, be explicit and direct with your students that every day you are going to give them a wonderful gift—the gift of time. Time to immerse themselves in text. Time to lose themselves in characters and their stories. Time to investigate their own wonders and find the answers to their burning questions. Students need to understand how precious this time is, and that we will protect it from everything from bathroom breaks, to book shopping, to reading response activities. This is time to read. The only thing you do during independent reading time is read!

2. Pledging to Read Outside of School

As we are developing the habit of daily reading in class, it is essential that we expect students to own this habit outside the walls of school. In classrooms we create the perfect conditions for students to engage in this worthwhile endeavor: we provide the time, space, and materials. We hand them these gifts on a silver platter! But if the reading habit is school- and teacher-dependent, do students own the habit? We believe the answer is no, not without the added expectation of developing the habit of reading on their own time. We know that daily reading in class benefits students; however, the case can be made that that is not enough time to develop the habits of a reader for most students. It is essential that students develop the routine of carving out the time and space in their at-home lives for reading; only this way will they become readers for life.

Referring back to the completed surveys communicates that the information that students provided is valuable, that it will be used for lessons and instruction, and to set personal reading goals (see page 73).

We know that students have a variety of activities they are committed to and engage in outside of school. We encourage you to examine completed student Reading Surveys (see page 35) and pay close attention to the responses to question 12: *I would read more if...* Chart all the things from the survey that get in the way of student reading. Using a show of hands, count the number of students for each response and record the total using tally marks on the chart. What do you notice? What are the things that get in the way of your students' reading? Next, investigate student responses to question 14: *How could you make more time for pleasure reading?* Are there commonalities among your students? Which ones are highly scheduled and therefore have less flexibility? Which ones are proficient time wasters?

Mary

When I reviewed student responses to question 14, I found most students indicated that they could make more time for reading if they watched less TV. This launched a great conversation with the class about how much viewing time is adequate and appropriate.

As teachers we must ensure that reading is on our students' nightly to-do list, along with the hockey practices, music lessons, and chores around their home. And we must try to get reading near the top! It's time for kids to make a pledge, a commitment to themselves to develop the habit of reading. Have your students formally pledge to read outside of school.

- Our friend Stephanie Cook created a Radical Reader card for her Grade 3 students that required them to read five out of seven nights a week for a specified length of time, which increased as year progressed. Parents recorded the length of time spent reading and initialed the card for each day. Completed cards were returned at the end of the month.
- In our Grade 6 classes, we ask students to pledge twenty minutes of reading, five out of seven days a week. Our intention is to develop a daily reading habit and to have students commit to reading a text long enough that they derive pleasure from the experience. This is an obligation and our daily homework expectation for students. See pages 77–78 for Pledge Card template.

To use the Pledge Card templates on pages 77–78, make double-sided copies of the pages and cut out the cards so the pledge is on one side and the list for titles read is on the other.

We're fooling ourselves if we think a one-size-fits-all approach is going to work for every student. Even if it works for the majority, there will be a few outliers for whom the expectation requires tweaking. As teachers we know that some students are overscheduled and have many home demands that interfere with their reading. For example, when Brittany returned her October pledge card, we were dismayed with how little time she was able to devote to the habit of reading. In a conference, Brittany disclosed that she was expected to babysit younger siblings three nights a week because her single mother did shift work. This led to a renegotiation of Brittany's pledge and a conversation about where she could find time. It's important to address the challenges that students may face finding time to read, and help them generate possible solutions.

Brittany's story is a perfect example of how a student's reading pledge can be used as fodder for reading conferences.

3. Permission to Pillage and Plunder

Knowing that students lead very busy lives opens the door to discussing the opportunity to pillage and plunder time—time that is not spent engaged in a specific activity; bits and pieces of time that float around our days, unaccounted for. Share various time scenarios with students that are relevant to their daily lives. For example:

> *This weekend you are going to a tournament that is two-and-a-half hours away. Have you considered what reading material you are going to take along for the journey? Don't waste that time!*
>
> *Your family is going for your annual dental cleaning. While your sister is getting her pearly whites checked, what are you doing? Watching the screens or reading outdated magazines? No! You are getting lost in your latest read.*

"I'm done!" How many times a day do you say or think that. Well, no need to ask me what you can do now, because these snippets of time can always be spent reading!

Consider at the end of each week having students brainstorm, or popcorn out, times and places they pillaged and plundered extra reading time. This can provide the entire class with ideas for when they can steal some extra time.

The Habit of Planning *Where*

So students know what they are going to read. They know when they are going to do it. But do they know where they will read outside of school? What specific places enable them to escape from it all and dive into a book without being distracted? Passionate readers can readily name their reading habitats.

> *Mary*
>
> During the day, my reading space it is the curled up on the living room couch. In the summer I can always be found rocking and reading on the front porch. At night it is snuggled under the covers in bed with my book.

Where is your reading space at home—a hammock in the backyard or an oversized chair in the den? Each of us has our favorite spots to read. For many, these spots have certain things in common. They are often quiet, comfortable, and cozy. As students grow as readers, they begin to establish reading nooks around their homes, places where they can relax and immerse themselves in text. You must support your developing readers as they uncover places where they can engage in reading, free from interruptions and distractions.

All the Places We Love to Read

Students will
- share and discover all the places they enjoy reading

A great way to launch a conversation about the places students enjoy reading is to read aloud the poem "Booktime" by Avis Harley, featured in the book *Falling down the Page* by Georgia Heard and reproduced on page 59. Harley's catchy poem celebrates all the places to read. From the beach to the treehouse, to the bus stop, places to read abound. After reading the poem, encourage your excited students to share all the wild and wacky places they love to read. Record student thinking on a chart.

Extension

Consider having groups of students work collaboratively to create their own "Booktime"-inspired poem.

Reprinted with permission of the author.

Booktime by Avis Harley

So many places to read a book—
bedroom
living room
kitchen nook

classroom
lunchroom
library
hall—
bus stop
treetop
hilltop
mall

backyard
garden
patio
park—
under-
the-sheets-
in-flash-lit-
dark

teahouse
treehouse
subway
train—
attic
camper
trailer
plane

seaside
lakeside
by a brook—
Where do you like to read your book?

Students will

- begin to realize that different people like reading in different places, and sometimes there are commonalities

Catch-a-Reader Photo Challenge

A fun and engaging way to celebrate the growing readers in your classroom is to catch them in the act! Surprise them by taking their photo while they are reading. Whether it is at their desk, on a pillow, under the blackboard, or in a corner, students seek their favorite spots to read around the room. Once you have developed these images and displayed them prominently in the classroom, encourage students to take note of other students and staff reading around the school. With a smart phone, disposable camera, or tablet, have your students become photographers and catch these readers. Add these photos to your display and watch it grow!

Extension

Consider having students capture images of their family caught reading and proudly display them on a bulletin board.

The Habit of Finding

Once students have uncovered their reading preferences in terms of genre, it is time they develop appropriate selection techniques. It is time for you to assist them in choosing a book that is a good fit, a book they are interested in and motivated to read. Have you ever reflected on how you select books? We took a trip to our local book store and decided to do some on-the-spot scientific research. We homed in on how readers of every age found text to read. We marveled at the vast array of selection behaviors exhibited. Some shoppers arrived with a list of specific titles they were longing for in hand. Others hunted for a particular author or the next in a series. Others seemed to be drawn to eye-catching displays and turned books over to read the back covers. Some created their own preview stacks and found an empty chair to sit and read the first few pages of each book. Students appear unaware of the many ways readers find their next read—a text that is appropriate in terms of reading level and content, but also one that they are excited by and want to read.

Anne

When I became librarian at my school, I was stunned to discover that most students had very few strategies for selecting text. I was shocked to see many students walk up and down the aisles, bent over to read the spines, as if that was the most effective way to find a book.

Becoming a Savvy Selector

Students will
- discover the various ways readers find text to read

One great way to show students the variety of selection strategies readers use to determine if a book is a good fit is to mine a cover for essential information. But instead of hitting the books immediately, engage students by beginning with an artifact they are familiar with—the breakfast of champions, cereal! Bring in a few boxes of cereal for your students to examine. Have them identify all the pieces of information they can gather from the box: e.g., cereal name, catchy slogan, brand, nutritional information, ingredients, maybe a recipe or an activity for children to complete. Students will be surprised by the amount of information presented on these relatively small boxes.

1. Get your students to think about a smaller package that contains even more vital information—a book! Select a text that has many of these features: title, author, illustrator, front jacket flap, back jacket, endorsements, and maybe an award seal. Take the time to draw students' attention to each of the features and deconstruct how they support the reader in deciding whether they will purchase the book/sign it out, or put it back on the shelf:

   When I was at Chapters the other day I was searching for my next read. As soon as I walked in, I was drawn to a book on display.

   Illustration: *The image of the moon on the front cover drew me in. I was mesmerized by the illustration of a young girl with windswept hair surrounded by birds that appeared to glow and a tiny dragon.*

   Title: *The title "The Girl Who Drank the Moon" was intriguing and made me wonder how that would even possible.*

   Genre: *From the illustration of the dragon and the title I predicted that this book might be in the fantasy genre.*

   Author: *Then I looked for the author and was excited to discover it was written by Kelly Barnhill, who wrote* The Witch's Boy, *a book I had previously enjoyed.*

   Book excerpt: *I quickly turned the book over and read a small intriguing excerpt "There is magic in starlight, of course. This is well known. Moonlight, however. That is a different story. Moonlight is magic. Ask anyone you like." I pondered what that meant and how that could connect with the story.*

   Endorsements: *As my eyes scanned the back cover I discovered seven endorsements from very reputable organizations, and five were accompanied by stars! As I read these recommendations certain words and phrases jumped off the page:* swiftly paced, highly imaginative plot, expertly woven and enchanting, utterly spellbinding.

   Inside jacket flap: *At this point I thought it was definitely worth opening up the book and reading the inside jacket. It would provide me a plot summary without giving away too much. After reading this interesting intro I was sold.*

2. In a short monologue, you have provided students with six features found on a book that influenced your decision to want to read and purchase this title. But you don't have to stop there.
   - Encourage students to discover the density of the text: how long is it, the amount of text on a page, the way in which the text is structured. It's vital for some students to know that the demands of the text are in line with their

stamina. A child who has typically read shorter chapter books should not be discouraged from longer texts, but must understand the commitment a lengthier text requires of them.

- You also want to motivate students to open the book. Remember our research trip to the local bookstore; many of the shoppers were reading the book as they stood in the store. So let's make sure our students know that a savvy selector reads prior to purchase.
- Steven Layne encourages teachers to draw students' attention to the one-sentence description of the entire story found in the cataloguing data on the copyright page. It is a succinct statement describing the gist of the story. Keep in mind some of these one-sentence summaries give away the ending.
- The back jacket flap may contain interesting author information, such as the URL for the author's website, Twitter handles, other titles, reviews, etc.

3. Create an anchor chart that outlines the various features used to support a reader in text selection.

Extension

Provide students with bins of books and have them practice being savvy selectors by using the features outlined above to choose their next read. They will quickly discover that not all books contain all the features mentioned; it depends on whether they are hard cover or paperback, and on the publisher. But even if some information is absent, they will know what features they can rely on to help make their book decision. This selection process should become a habit for all readers. We believe this is a lesson that bears repeating throughout the year as students fully develop their repertoire of selection strategies.

Just Dance

Students will
- discover the importance of selecting text in their independent-reading range

Anne

At the cottage on a rainy day, my nieces challenged me to a dance-off using the Xbox game *Just Dance*. The girls quickly selected a level and the competition began—with disastrous results. It was clear within the first few steps that the level of the game was well above my ability and I was sure to lose the battle. The sequence of steps was too complex and too fast, and I was unable to keep up. I was ready to throw in the towel and take a seat on the couch as a spectator, since I was having zero fun. But instead I advocated for myself and pleaded with the girls to lower the level and select something less intense. I knew that if I stayed at this difficult level I wasn't going to get better; I was going to quit to save face. Well, they lowered the level to the opposite extreme, Level One. To say it was boring was an understatement. I could follow along with ease but I wasn't learning any new moves. This was in no way going to make me a better dancer. So I had the girls advance the game a few levels till we found something that was just right—I could do the majority of the steps, I was able to keep up, and yet I was still learning some new moves while having fun. Experiencing a measure of success made the activity more enjoyable.

Isn't this just like reading, especially when reading on your own? You want to select a text that is just right—one you are able to read with a high level of *accuracy*, *comprehension*, and *enjoyment* (*ACE*). Sadly, many students have adopted the belief that harder is better. In their minds, harder is directly linked to the lack of illustrations, the thickness of the book, and the number of pages. It would appear our super-size–obsessed culture has made its way into reading. Some students are willing to sacrifice accuracy, comprehension, and enjoyment to pretend to read "hard" books. Anne was unable to fake her ability to dance proficiently at level 8, but some students do this every day in classrooms. They pick up texts that they have difficulty reading, they struggle through without comprehending, and return them to the library, having not read it at all, but proclaiming "This was a good book." And then parents wonder why their children are not improving as readers. But we know why: they are spending precious time reading text that is not just right.

1. Take this analogy to the classroom and fire up the *Just Dance* video. I'm sure you will have no problem getting a few volunteers from your class to put on their dancing shoes and demonstrate the range of ability that exists within the room. Be sure to put yourself out there and model the struggle a less-proficient dancer has doing this activity. (Even if you are the reigning *Just Dance* Champion at home, play along for today!)
2. Use questions, statements, prompts as discussion points:
   - *Were you surprised that we all weren't at the same level?*
   - *When did you know that the level was just right for you?* (You could do the majority of the steps, you were able to keep up, and yet you were still learning some new moves while having fun.)
   - *When the level didn't match your ability, how did you feel?* (Too Difficult: frustrated, embarrassed, wanted to quit; Too Easy: bored, uninterested)
   - *What made you so proficient at this game?* (They probably will disclose that they have the video game at home, have spent hours practicing, or even take dance lessons.)
   - *What do you think I need to do to become better at this game?* (Students will likely share that you need more practice time. Deconstruct what is meant by practice to ensure that students understand that we would gradually increase the level of difficulty to improve.)

3. Connect the ideas discussed to reading:
   - Will every reader in this class be at the same level?
   - What makes a book just right?
   - How do you feel when a book does not match your ability? When it is too difficult? Too easy?
   - How does a reader become more proficient?

4. Explain to students that when selecting text, they are expected to ask themselves the following question: *Can I* ACE *this book?* In the classroom, this means

   Can I read this text with a high degree of **A**ccuracy?

   Am I able to **C**omprehend the story and events/information?

   Am I deriving **E**njoyment and pleasure from this text?

If a student is able to answer yes to these three questions, then they have a selected a text they can *ACE*! These questions should become part of every reading conference, as they clearly communicate a student's ability to find appropriate text.

Speed Dating Books

Students will
- practice using their selection skills to choose a book they can *ACE*

A wonderful way to engage and hook students in practicing being savvy selectors and discovering books they can *ACE* is to use the popular technique of speed dating.

1. Connect with your school librarian and work together to create bountiful baskets of books; be sure that there is an abundant supply of titles to keep students engaged. Strategically select texts you are confident will tempt your reluctant readers based on information they provided on their interest surveys. Each basket should be filled with a variety of genres, levels, topics, and formats. Depending on the size of groups, you'll want to make certain that there are more books than students in each group.
2. Before "dating" commences, review the savvy selector techniques (page 61) and what it takes to *ACE* a book (page 63) to support students in finding just right titles.
3. Distribute a Next-Read list to each student so students can keep track of the texts they want to read in the future. See template on page 79.
4. Provide students with an appropriate amount of time to peruse their basket and apply the selection techniques explored. Some educators have used a timer to mimic actual speed dating, but we suggest that you refrain from doing this so that students don't feel pressured and rushed to make a decision prematurely. You want them to take their time and utilize all their selection skills.
5. While students are busy examining texts, be a keen observer and offer support where needed. If you notice a student is switching books quickly or not recording any titles, this indicates they require more direction and support from you, the lead reader.

The Habit of Acting: Thinking

As we set out to create a reading community, it is imperative that we take the temperature of the room and find out how students define reading. What is their working definition? Do they describe a reader as someone who can pronounce all the words accurately, is fluent, attends to punctuation, is expressive, and reads at a good pace? Yes, these are characteristics of a proficient reader, but do they know that there is much more? You need to ask the question: *What is reading?*

Reading Is... Snowball

Students will
- share and grow their definition of reading

Initially, many developing readers have a very narrow definition of reading. They pay attention to the overt actions and are less aware of the covert; i.e., what happens inside the reader's head and heart that is unseen. Our readers must become acquainted with the thinking that goes along with reading, the invisible actions that take place in their brain that contribute to reading.

1. Distribute slips of paper divided into two equal sections with the sentence stem *Reading is...* in each half. Students complete the sentences anonymously.

2. Once students have documented their thinking about reading, they gather in a circle. Students crumple their papers into balls and toss them into the centre of the circle.
3. Each student scoops up a "snowball" and shares the first response with the whole group.
4. After everyone has had a chance to share, re-toss the snowballs and repeat the process again. This time students read the second response on the slip of paper.
5. Slips of paper are passed to the teacher, who re-crumples, rolls, and tapes them together into a large lump that represents the Reading Brain.
6. The teacher reviews a variety of responses and consolidates the thinking of the class:

> *If we were to summarize all of the responses we shared today, I wonder what we would say? Is there a common idea that represents what reading is? READING IS THINKING!*

The Reading Conversation

Students will
- be introduced to the concept of annotating text through a think-aloud

In *Strategies that Work,* Harvey and Goudvis detail the thinking routine they call Leaving Tracks of Thinking and Inner Conversation, while Chris Tovani calls this strategy "annotating the text." Whatever you choose to call it, the process involves paying attention to the thinking taking place while reading to make meaning.

1. Introduce the concept:

> *Did you know that each and every time you pick up a piece of text, you and the book are actually having a conversation? An inner discussion is taking place inside your head. I wonder what you are saying? What you are thinking? Have you ever considered that you are talking with the text the entire time you are reading? I see that some of you are shaking your heads.*
>
> *Today we're going to try to listen to what your reading brain has to say. While I'm reading aloud, I am going to open up my reading brain and let you hear what I'm thinking inside my head. I'm going to jot down my thinking on these sticky notes. So let's start…*

Picture books we have used successfully to explore deeper thinking with students:
Those Shoes by Maribeth Boelts
Ish by Peter Reynolds
Goal! by Mina Javaherbin
The Most Magnificent Thing by Ashley Spires
Leah's Pony by Elizabeth Friedrich
My Name Is Blessing by Eric Walters
The Can Man by Laura E. Williams
Migrant by Maxine Trottier

Selecting Text that Promotes Thinking

Before you grab the sticky notes, let's explore the importance of text selection. When our goal is to have students think deeply and talk intentionally about books, we must ensure that we are reading text that is thought-provoking. So choose books with intention and care. Allan Luke suggests selecting topics that are intellectually demanding, promote sustained classroom conversation, and are rich enough to provide a big idea that connects the reader to the world (Luke, 2014). We use this criteria to select text that allows us to entertain this type of deep-thinking during a read-aloud. When deciding if a text has merit, consider the following questions:

- What thinking is taking place inside my head?

- What reading comprehension strategies heighten my interaction and engagement while reading?
- In what ways has my heart been touched, stimulated, or moved?
- How has my thinking been validated, changed, or expanded?
- How have I been inspired or called on to think and act differently after reading this text?
- What message/moral/life lesson/big idea am I taking with me from this text?

2. While reading the text aloud to students, stop at strategic points in the text to model your inner conversation. Demonstrate the variety of thinking taking place in your reading brain as you attempt to make meaning of and comprehend the text. For example, share the questions you are asking, the background knowledge you are drawing on; jot down your predictions, inferences, and connections; etc.
3. A rich read-aloud provides the perfect time for students to tap into their thinking and calls on them to talk. After a few pages of modeling your thinking, encourage students to turn-and-talk and share their thoughts with a peer. By engaging in a common text experience and being required to share their thinking with peers, the solitary act of reading is turned into a social one.

Since the process of using a read-aloud to annotate text slows down the reading, usually the story will not be finished in one sitting. This builds anticipation among students and fosters contemplation with the text.

4. Continue the lesson in a second reading. Briefly review what was read.
5. Provide students with their own thinking sheet or sticky notes on which to jot down their inner conversation.
6. Continue reading aloud. Stop at strategic points to foster thinking opportunities for students. Encourage them to not censor themselves and to jot down exactly what they are thinking.

The purpose of intentionally selecting student ideas to share is to honor student thinking, to draw connections within the thinking in the class, and to label students' thinking. We want our readers to understand that they think while they read, that at times our thinking is similar and different from one another's, and that monitoring our inner conversation cements our reading relationship with the text.

7. After the reading, collect and review those tracks of thinking so that you can see their inner conversation with the text (i.e., questioning, predictions, comments, connections, inferences, etc.).
8. Select different tracks to use for discussion. Look for similarities in thinking; Did a number of students pose the same question? If so, share that:

   Max, Raja, Miriam, and Charlie all asked a similar question, which was…

   See if any students have linked their thinking to their background knowledge. Share that too. Give voice to the thinking of students who have made predictions or offered insightful inferences. Reveal thinking that is unique, surprising, and profound.

The Reading Brain

Students will
- explore the various comprehension strategies readers use to make meaning

Since your readers are now aware that an intimate conversation occurs in their mind when they read, it's time to recognize the variety of comprehension strategies they use in their Reading Brain. The Reading Brain graphic on page 80 is a tangible way to make the invisible workings of the brain visible. Display it in a place of prominence so that it can be referred to frequently and provide an anchor for conversation.

1. Using the thinking generated and recorded during The Reading Conversation lesson on page 65, gather examples of the various strategies readers used to make meaning.
2. Share the strategies with the class, labeling the thinking strategy and celebrating the array of thinking taking place within your room:

The delight of having their thinking validated and shared publicly will be clear on students' faces.

Wow, Tia, you asked a ton of questions as a reader.

(Share specific questions.)

Parker, you made a number of comments on what was taking place in the text such as...

(Share text analysis)

Talal, it's clear you have background knowledge and tapped into that while I was reading to help you make meaning.

3. Spotlight a specific reader who has recorded a variety of thinking, focusing on the different strategies the reader used to comprehend, to demonstrate that comprehending is a very complex process. Students will also come to understand that there are similarities and differences among readers in terms of the kinds of thinking they do.
4. Introduce the Reading Brain graphic to identify or review the reading comprehension strategies that readers use. Review the thinking of one student with the class, tracking the kinds of thinking they did on the Reading Brain.

> Mary: I use magnets on the particular parts of the brain a reader used.
> Anne: I created an interactive whiteboard file.

Whatever technique you choose, be sure to celebrate student thinking and communicate to students that their thinking matters.

6. Spotlight a number of readers to demonstrate the variety of thinking.

Extension

During independent reading time, have students track the types of thinking they do while reading by coloring in parts of the Reading Brain as they identify the strategies they are using. See the Reading Brain Exit Ticket template on page 81. As they color in particular sections over several days, students will begin to note which strategies they use frequently and which they rarely use, and to contemplate whether this is related to the type of text they are reading.

The Habit of Acting: Talking

Thinking and Talking—In a reading classroom, you can't have one without the other!

Real readers talk about books. They gravitate toward each other. They long to talk about characters, their actions and decisions. They're eager to share their wonderings before, during, and after reading. However, students often enter the classroom unaware that talking about text is an essential component of the reading experience. You know what we're talking about—you ask students to speak with an elbow partner and all you hear is crickets! We wonder why this is. Is it that they don't believe their responses are valued? Or is it that they are rarely asked to share their thinking? Do we as teachers dominate classroom talk? Are we not waiting long enough for them to formulate a response? Or perhaps they have discovered that they can wait us out and we'll provide the answer. But not in a reading classroom. Students will learn that in a reading classroom, their responses are valued. In a reading classroom they will be continually asked to share their thinking. We will wait long enough for them to formulate a response. And the void will not be filled by us. We want to hear them. As James Britton has said, "reading and writing must float on a sea of talk" (Britton, 1970). So let's get students talking.

Sharing your thinking orally requires you to articulate it in a clear and coherent manner. Talking requires you to synthesize, summarize, and consolidate your thinking. For students who have always seen reading as a solitary experience, this opens up a whole new reading habit. Readers talk. And if students have rarely been expected to share their thinking orally, their initial attempts will be disjointed, stunted, and superficial. If you model authentic "reader talk" and make time daily for your students to practice, they will begin to develop the crucial habit of talking about books. They will also begin to recognize that what drives their reading experience is the relationship between reader and text. The active thinking taking place while reading is what fosters engagement, as it supports their immersion in the story and keeps them reading. The rewards of talking about text are endless:

- it creates bonds among readers
- it deepens student comprehension
- it broadens our perspective by exposing us to different viewpoints
- it enables us to learn to accept differences in opinion
- our background is augmented by the thinking of others
- it allows the teacher to push and move students to deeper thinking
- it provides teachers with the opportunity to assess student thinking on the fly

Indeed, conversation is the fuel for our reading community.

The Habit of Acting: Sharing

There is no doubt about it; readers act in habitual ways. They think, they talk, and they share. Reading communities thrive on opportunities for students to share their enthusiasm, their passion, and their joy for books. Just as providing daily independent reading time allows students to develop their reading stamina and immerse themselves in text, providing sharing time for developing readers is vital. Sharing time enables students to sell one another on books, to find their next read, to be inspired and motivated by their classmates. At the beginning of the year the lead reader (That's you!) takes on the primary role of sharing. We encourage you to:

- spotlight an author
- highlight a particular genre
- share a favorite series
- sell students on particular titles
- present magazine or newspaper articles

Sharing needs to be frequent and varied so that students develop a bank of ways they can share when the responsibility is shifted to them. Formal and informal sharing opportunities take place in an active reading community. For example, students may sign up to present a Book Bite to the class; after independent reading you might ask students to share their current read and how they made their selection. Keep the sharing organic, having students share in a variety of ways with an assortment of discussion points.

Formal Sharing Techniques

Book Bite

Kelly Gallagher calls it a Reading Minute, Penny Kittle a Book Talk, Donalyn Miller a Book Commercial—we call a short talk about a book a Book Bite. The essence of each of these strategies is the same; we're talking to persuade others to read a featured book. Our friend Charmaine Graves would say that this sharing opportunity should be "short, sharp, and shiny." We expect students to include the following elements:

- title
- author
- genre
- gist statement
- identification of characters by name
- a sales pitch for the book
- a suggestion of who in the class might like to read the text.

No spoilers allowed.

As we build our reading community, each student is expected to sign up and do a Book Bite on a book they have read independently during the school year. After everyone has had an opportunity to formally share, students who finish text and are interested are encouraged to sign up on the Book Bite calendar.

Gold Star Books

Another strategy that will support the development of your reading community is celebrating the readers in your room by spotlighting them. Feature a reader in the class for a week: the student is photographed on a Friday and asked to reflect and select three or four pieces of text they deem to be gold-star quality—interesting, engaging, thought-provoking, a must-read. On the following Monday, start with a flattering introduction of the featured reader. Share all the wonderful things you have uncovered about them; consider referring to their reader survey, their I Am a Reader Who… poem, and reading conferences. After pumping them up in front of the class, ask them to reveal each of their Gold Star books. Prominently display these titles with the student's photograph. Over the next few days, have the student share and justify why they believe each text deserves a gold star. Record title, author, and student recommender on a die-cut star to build a classroom bank of Gold Star texts. You can keep the stars in a bin so that students can refer to them for text selection support: often simply reading the old star jogs a student's memory; the recommender might be called upon to provide more information weeks after the fact.

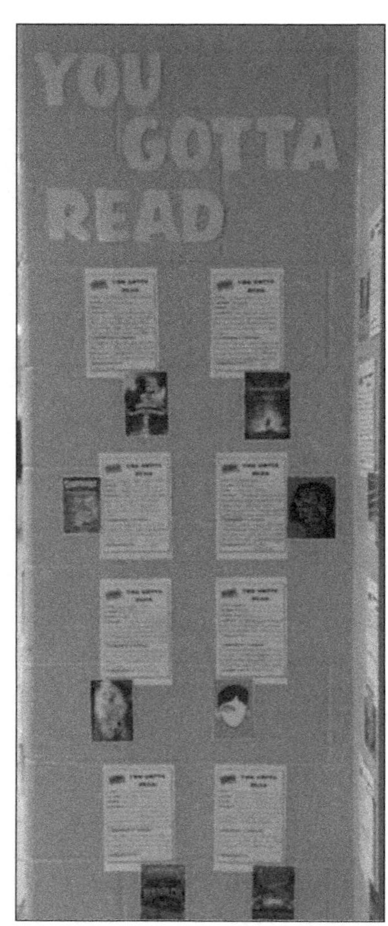

You Gotta Read... Cards

Sometimes we like to move beyond our classroom to make our reading lives public to others. Sharing with the broader school community communicates to other staff and students that we value reading. On a card (see You Gotta Read... Cards template on page 82), students are asked to identify the title, author, and genre of their chosen text, to provide a brief summary (five lines), and to complete the sentence stem: *I recommend it because....* Invest time in modeling how to craft a short summary without revealing too much of the story: draw students' attention to the CIP page for the one-line summary to provide a starting point for their writing; use the book jacket recommendations to generate an anchor chart of colorful phrases that can be used in their recommendations (e.g., *a real page turner, a must-read, kept me on the edge of my seat, read with a Kleenex, action-packed story, heart-warming narrative, mind-blowing read, laugh-out- loud funny*). Post the cards alongside images of the text covers in the hall. You will be amazed at the buzz this display will generate among other students.

Informal Sharing Techniques

#IMWAYR

One significant way to invest in building a reading community is to ensure that we flood the classroom with talk about our current reads. Many of you are probably familiar with the hashtag on Twitter #IMWAYR (It's Monday, What Are You Reading), which has since been modified by many Twitter users. This hashtag is the perfect addition to Monday routines, as it leads to impromptu conversations among small groups of classmates about their reading. Tossing out the phrase "It's Monday, What Are You Reading?" sparks natural talk about books and leads students to make their reading life public to one another. It facilitates authentic, free-flowing conversation in which students share, ask questions, swap titles, and get to know each other as readers without the teacher driving the dialogue.

#IFWDYR

Similar to starting Monday conversations, on Friday give students an opportunity to recap and review what they have read throughout the week with It's Friday, What Did You Read? It's a great chance for you to pick up any tidbits from the ensuing conversations: Who really can "sell" their book? Who asks questions of their peers? Who appears to be genuinely interested and invested in the talk? Who writes something down on their Next-Read list? This quick, simple activity allows you to make key observations about your developing readers.

Buzzing About Books

When you create the routine to buzz/talk about books, students cannot be silenced. The habit has clearly been established and they come to take ownership for this talk time. In our classrooms we never ask our students to read during Independent Reading time without providing them with the opportunity to talk afterward. Once the routine becomes ingrained, omitting this time risks the wrath of the readers in your room! Here are a few of our favorite Buzzing about Books prompts:

- Describe the main character of your story. Use details.

- Which character would you like to have as a friend? Explain why.
- If you had the opportunity to meet with a character from your story, what questions would you ask?
- How does the setting play an important part in your story?
- Explain what the author has done to hook you as a reader and move the story along?
- Describe a decision the main character made and tell how it affected the plot.
- What do you think is going to happen next in the story? Why do you think this?
- Describe your book. Is it a fast-paced page turner, slow and steady, or tedious?
- What twists and turns has the author led you on?
- Why do you think the author wrote this story?
- If you could ask the author a question, what would you ask?
- Give three words to describe your story. (May be followed with the expectation that students justify their word choice).

Next-Read Lists

Whether you keep it on your phone, in a special notepad, or scrawled on scraps of paper, readers keep Next-Read lists. A friend recommends a book, you hear a title that intrigues you on CBC radio, your favorite blogger is raving about a book, or you read a captivating review in a magazine while at the hair salon—and you are compelled to jot down the title. These ever-growing lists become a library patron's or book shopper's best friend when you go to select your next read. Simulate the same experience in your classroom by providing your students with their own Next-Read lists. You can distribute the template on page 79 photocopied on card stock or simply give them large, lined sticky notes. It is important to keep the list in a safe and reliable place so that it can be easily accessed. Next-Read lists will make book shopping focused and intentional.

The Habit of Setting Goals

As adults, each and every one of us sets and attempts to accomplish goals on a daily, weekly, yearly, or even lifelong basis. Anne has a daily goal to drink six glasses of water. Mary has a weekly goal to visit the gym three times. Our friend Jane Baird is working toward reading sixty books in a year. Mary and Anne both have the lifelong goal of going on safari in Kenya (which we plan to have crossed off our list in 2018). Our goals drive our thoughts, actions, and routines. Think about a personal goal you have; it can be as simple as packing a healthy lunch each day or as grand as hiking up Mount Kilimanjaro. Consider the commitment, planning, and sacrifices you may have to make in order to achieve your goal. It takes effort and energy, determination and perseverance to reach any goal.

In our classrooms it is no different. We craft many goals with our students: learning skills, behavior, subject-area expectations, and more. These goals are set; however, without being monitored by student or teacher, it's not a surprise that they are rarely met. When setting goals with students, we cannot adopt the slow-cooker mentality of setting them and forgetting them. We must support students as they set, monitor, and reflect on their goals.

In our reading classrooms, we want to create the habit of setting specific, manageable goals. But it's been our experience that students have difficulty doing this when left to their own devices. How often have you witnessed a student draft a reading goal that is incredibly vague—*Read harder books*, *Read different genres*—or goals are totally unrealistic—*Read 10 novels a month*? These ineffective goals stem from our students' lack of awareness of the many elements that contribute to a person being a passionate and proficient reader. They are not mindful of their own strengths and areas of need as readers, which in turn leads them to randomly formulate goals that are vague and unrealistic. Students seem to pull them from out of thin air, eagerly set them, and quickly forget them. However, if you have invested time in developing the first three habits—Plan, Find and Act—then you have frontloaded the knowledge students need to be able to craft a specific goal.

Passionate/Proficient Reader Anchor Chart

Students will

- work collaboratively to build an anchor chart that outlines characteristics of a passionate and proficient reader

We have worked diligently to reveal the habits of real readers to our students through the Plan, Find, and Act activities. Now is the time to discover what students have internalized and committed to memory. Prepare yourself to be impressed!

1. Begin by asking your students to think about the following prompt: *What characteristics make a passionate and proficient reader?* Encourage students to share their thinking with an elbow partner.
2. Once they have had an opportunity to brainstorm together, have students brainstorm or popcorn out their ideas while you record their thinking on chart paper. Characteristics your students might suggest based on the habits of readers might lead to an anchor chart like this sample:

Passionate Readers...	*Proficient Readers...*
• dedicate time to read • read daily • make a reading schedule • plan what they are going to read • use their interests and preferences to select text (i.e., genre, topics, series, author) • are never without a book • read different types of texts (e.g., books, magazines, websites) • have favorite spots to read • preview books carefully • keep a Next-Read list • talk about their reading with other readers • get lost in text (i.e., have stamina) • share recommendations with other readers	• know that reading is thinking • leave tracks • use a variety of thinking strategies • hook into their background knowledge • select books using the ACE technique • read different genres • carry on an inner conversation when they read • can identify the thinking strategies they use most often or prefer • think about characters, setting, plot, author's craft, author's purpose, big ideas

This list is by no means an exhaustive one. Your students will likely come up with many more ideas linked to oral reading skills, such as pace, fluency, expression, decoding strategies, fix-it strategies, etc.

Setting a Reading Goal

Students will

- watch as their teacher models setting a specific and manageable reading goal connected to a plan of action and indicators of success, using the co-constructed anchor chart

Modeling the creation of specific and manageable goals that match the readers in the room is imperative. It reveals to students the time, effort, and energy that must be put into creating an appropriate goal. So let's demonstrate the thought process a reader goes through when crafting a fitting goal.

1. Start with your own goal by using the co-constructed Passionate/Proficient Reader anchor chart from page 72. Your conversation with students might go something like this:

    Yesterday we created this extensive anchor chart that outlines all the things we know a passionate, proficient reader does. But to be honest, I'm not sure I do all those things consistently and thoughtfully

    (At this point you might take time with your class to tease out what "consistently" and "thoughtfully" mean to the students you teach.)

    So today I want to read over the chart and identify all the things I think I do consistently and thoughtfully.

    (Place a colored sticky note beside each characteristic that describes you as a reader on the anchor chart. As you examine the characteristics, think out loud and justify your *Yes*es and your *Nos*.)

    For example, I do commit to daily reading, every night before I go to bed. I do recommend and swap titles regularly with my book-reading friends. I also keep a Next-Read list on my phone so that when I go to Chapters I have specific titles I can search for. Oh, I see something here that I don't do very often. It says here on the chart that passionate and proficient readers read many different genres. That's not me. I don't often branch out beyond my favorite genres. For example, I rarely read science fiction. I wonder how often I miss out on a wonderful read by always choosing realistic fiction, fantasy, and historical fiction. This could be a goal for me.

    This think-aloud process is vital in making students understand the inner dialogue that we want them to have with themselves as they reflect on themselves as readers. This informal data will be used to set their own reading goal.
2. Distribute copies of the anchor chart for individual students to use as a tool to reflect on their own reader characteristics. Direct students to pencil a checkmark beside the characteristics they do consistently and thoughtfully, while penciling a star beside two characteristics they think make an appropriate goal.
3. Re-gather students so that they can watch closely as you model creating a plan of action for a goal that is specific and manageable:

    I am really proud that I know my genre reading preferences: realistic fiction, fantasy, and historical fiction. But I've heard people mention some really great science fiction that I have not read, and it's got me thinking that I might be missing out on something. So I am going to set my goal as follows: Read a science fiction novel.

Note that this is where wheels often fall off the bus. Students typically do not devise a plan of action. They don't think through the specific steps they need to take to meet their goal. Continue to specify your plan of action:

> *I think the perfect place to find a science fiction novel is to ask my friends and I know just the person. My plan is to ask Wendy for a great title. I will also ask our school librarian for recommendations and I will browse our classroom library basket using my savvy selector skills. From those recommendations I will make my selection. I will keep this book on my bedside table and read it before bed each night. I will also post a reminder of my goal on my desk and on my bathroom mirror. My goal is to have this science fiction novel read by (specify date).*

Extension

You need to support each student in setting an appropriate, specific, and manageable goal with a concrete plan of action. This requires you to sit one-on-one and conference with each student. Working alongside students will pay huge dividends in getting to know the readers in your class, seeing connections between them, planning your reading mini-lessons, and, most importantly, setting up your readers for success. We acknowledge that these reading conferences will take time. But without this essential step to support our developing readers, we will end up with a slow-cooker of unmet goals that students will set and forget. To ensure this doesn't happen, check in frequently with readers to monitor their progress; see page 83 for a Reading Goal bookmark that will serve as a tool to remind them daily of their goal. As students develop the habit of setting goals, achieving them, and drafting new ones, you may find that the level of support students require of you decreases.

Genre Labels

Nonfiction	**Biography**
Realistic Fiction	**Historical Fiction**
Science Fiction	**Fantasy**
Mystery	

Genre Characteristics

• text involves information that is considered true • text informs the reader and may include information on a variety of topics	• nonfictional text about a real person's life • an auto______________ is when a person writes about his/her own life
• the story is one that could really happen • the story takes place in the present time	• the setting of the story is a period of time in the past; for example, medieval times or the 20th century
• the story involves science or futuristic technology • the setting could be in the future, in space, or in another universe	• the story includes elements that are not real, but are totally imagined • the story could involve some kind of magic
• the story involves a character investigating a mysterious or strange event or events • the secret is not solved until the end of the story	

Pledge Cards: Front

Reading Pledge

Month: ____________________

20 ______

S	M	T	W	TH	F	S

Monthly Reading Pledge Expectations

1. Read an ACE book.
2. Read the equivalent of 20 minutes per night, five out of seven nights per week.
3. Record the number of minutes you read each night.
4. Keep track of the titles and authors of the books you finish on the back of this card.
5. On the first day of next month, return your Reading Pledge Card to school.

Student's Name: ____________________

Parent's Signature: ____________________

Reading Pledge

Month: ____________________

20 ______

S	M	T	W	TH	F	S

Monthly Reading Pledge Expectations

1. Read an ACE book.
2. Read the equivalent of 20 minutes per night, five out of seven nights per week.
3. Record the number of minutes you read each night.
4. Keep track of the titles and authors of the books you finish on the back of this card.
5. On the first day of next month, return your Reading Pledge Card to school.

Student's Name: ____________________

Parent's Signature: ____________________

* Insert dates in calendar appropriate to the current month.

Pledge Cards: Back

Titles and Authors of Books Read
1. ______________________
2. ______________________
3. ______________________
4. ______________________
5. ______________________
6. ______________________
7. ______________________
8. ______________________
9. ______________________
10. ______________________

Titles and Authors of Books Read
1. ______________________
2. ______________________
3. ______________________
4. ______________________
5. ______________________
6. ______________________
7. ______________________
8. ______________________
9. ______________________
10. ______________________

Next-Read List

Title	Author

The Reading Brain

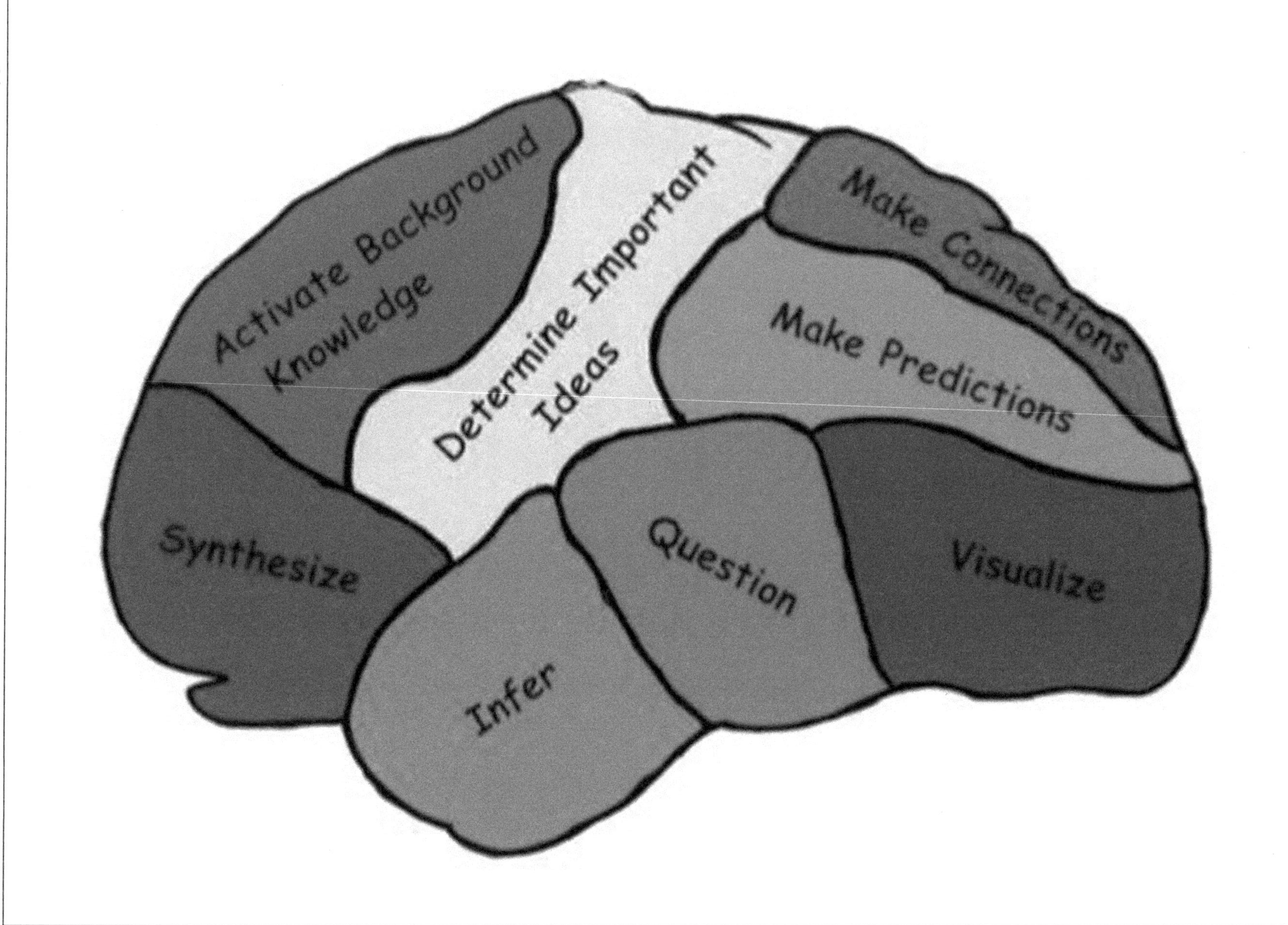

Pembroke Publishers ©2017 *Cultivating Readers* by Anne Elliott and Mary Lynch ISBN 978-1-55138-324-8

The Reading Brain Exit Ticket

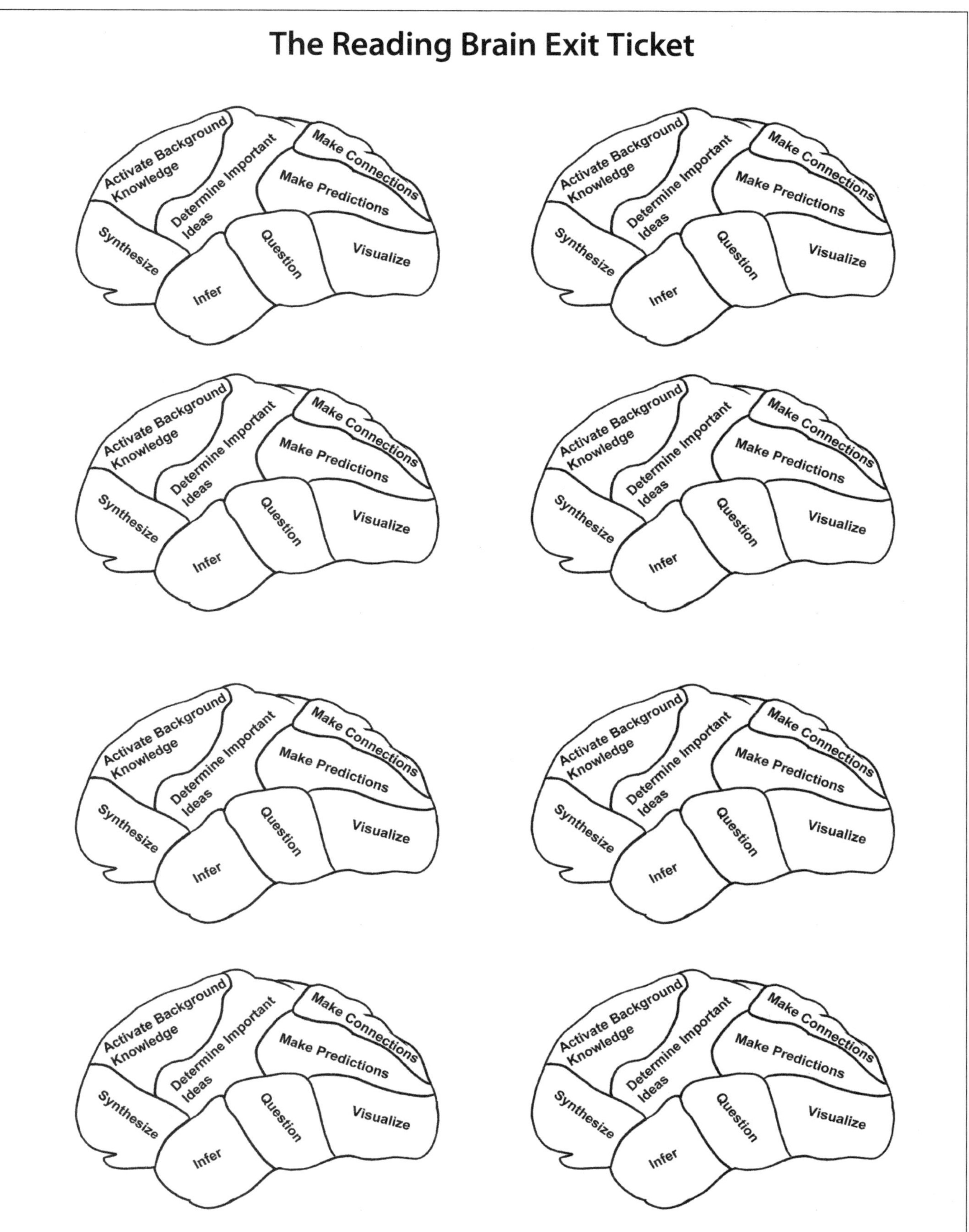

Pembroke Publishers ©2017 *Cultivating Readers* by Anne Elliott and Mary Lynch ISBN 978-1-55138-324-8

You Gotta Read… Cards

You Gotta Read…

Title: ______________________

Author: ______________________

Genre: ______________________

Summary: ______________________

____

____

____

____

____

I recommend it because ______________________

____

Recommended by ______________________

You Gotta Read…

Title: ______________________

Author: ______________________

Genre: ______________________

Summary: ______________________

____

____

____

____

____

I recommend it because ______________________

____

Recommended by ______________________

Pembroke Publishers ©2017 *Cultivating Readers* by Anne Elliott and Mary Lynch ISBN 978-1-55138-324-8

Reading Goal Bookmarks

Habits of a Reader

PLAN what, where, and when you will read.

FIND an *ACE* book.

ACT on your reading by thinking, talking, or writing about what you have read.

SET reading goals.

________________**'s Reading Goal:**

To become a better reader, I will...

____

____

____

____

____

____

Habits of a Reader

PLAN what, where, and when you will read.

FIND an *ACE* book.

ACT on your reading by thinking, talking, or writing about what you have read.

SET reading goals.

________________**'s Reading Goal:**

To become a better reader, I will...

____

____

____

____

____

____

5

Fourth Step: Making the *Why* of Reading Visible

Combined, we have 46 years of teaching experience. In that time we have attended countless conferences, ministry sessions, workshops, after-school make-and-takes, lunch-and-learns—and who could forget all the staff meetings we sat through? At each and every one of these sessions we have been at the receiving end of some form of professional development. Many of these events we have chosen to attend, while others have been mandated. Does this sound familiar? At each of these sessions you've probably sat at a table group of colleagues; if we were betting women, we could win money by predicting the variety of people at that table with you:

- The Presenter Pleasers walk out with a sore neck at the end of the session due to non-stop head-nodding in agreement. They are quick to jump onto bandwagons and implement the newest craze without question.
- At the other extreme, Negative Ned and Nellie are perpetual naysayers. No matter the speaker, topic, or evidence, the answer is always cynicism.
- Thankfully, the majority of us are Critical Consumers. We are open-minded and willing to entertain new ideas, new ways of teaching and learning. We thrive on conversation and dialogue with others that pushes our thinking, actions, and practice. When presented with something novel and new, our immediate response is neither "Yea" nor "Nay"; rather, we take the time to sit back and ponder, question, wonder, and consider fresh ideas. As Critical Consumers, we are anxious and eager to understand the relevancy of initiatives that ask us to change and modify our practice. We expect to be swayed, won over, and convinced. More often than not we need to understand the *why* before we act differently. For us it takes
    - educational research
    - personal testimonials of colleagues and friends
    - presenter power
    - literacy-leader name-dropping

Together these aspects of a presentation work to shift our thinking and change our practice by making the *why* visible to us.

Why Read?

As classroom teachers we are faced with the same challenge of having to sway, persuade, and convince our students that reading is worthwhile. We, too, have to make the *why* visible to them so that they shift their thinking and adopt new habits. Typically we have merely told students that reading is important without providing any evidence and justification for this statement. Is it any surprise that many do not truly believe that reading is important and therefore do not see the point in becoming committed readers? It is our responsibility to provide students with research they can understand and relate to, and personal reader testimonials that will inspire and influence them (e.g., from parents, teachers, principals, instructional coaches, etc.). As well, as the lead reader, we must continuously deconstruct the vague message that reading is important into specific explanations that answer the question "Why read?"

When making the *why* of reading visible to our students, we need to strike a balance between showing and telling. Students benefit from hearing the sales pitch from the presenter or lead reader—that's us. We passionately communicate to them the range of reasons that reading is important, valuable, and beneficial to them. But we cannot do this by merely telling; we must create learning experiences that show them. Back in 2002, Kelly Gallagher did just that for middle- and high-school students. Based on nine real-world reading reasons, he created a variety of lessons to show and tell. His work inspired us to reflect on how we could convey a more age-appropriate message to our younger students. Through our work in classrooms these reading reasons have emerged year after year:

- We read for pleasure and enjoyment.
- We read to increase our background knowledge and to learn more about topics.
- We read to become better writers.
- We read to expand our vocabulary.
- We read to learn valuable life lessons.

I Am the Book

Students will
- begin to identify reasons to read based on poems from *I Am the Book* (selected by Lee Bennett Hopkins)

Students have a very narrow perception of why reading is important. It's time to expand their lens and have them consider the many reasons why reading is important in their lives. Think of it like a zoom feature on a camera—this lesson will facilitate students in zooming out and focusing in on the many motives for reading.

1. Using the text *I Am the Book*, select a variety of poems to read aloud to your class that illustrate various reasons to read. The power of the poems is that they are fun to read, sound beautiful to the ear, and have illustrations that enhance the text. These whimsical poems have universal appeal and present many reasons to read, thinly veiled and waiting to be discovered. We have experienced success with many of these poems, including: "Wander Through the Pages" by Karla Kuskin, "What Was That?" by Rebecca Kay Dotlich, "Don't Need a Window Seat" by Kristine O'Connell George, and "I Am the Book" by Tom Robert Shields.

By actively engaging in the reading of each poem, your students will discover that reading is pleasurable to the tongue and ear.

2. As you read each selection aloud, have students decipher from the poem reasons to read. For example, from the lines of "Wander Through the Pages" by Karla Kuskin, students determined:
   - We read to learn ("knowledge came tumbling out")

- We travel through time ("histories shout")
- We go on adventures ("whispering mysteries," "wisdom of wizards")

3. Consider posing the following questions as prompts:
   - What is the author suggesting reading will do for us?
   - What benefits do we gain by being a reader?
   - What am I learning about reading from this poem?

Extension

Each day, choose a poem or two to investigate as a class. Track student thinking on a chart.

Reading for Pleasure

Our dear friend Stephanie Cook is a food lover. Going out for dinner with her is always an entertaining experience. From the moment she orders her drink, she starts to salivate over the menu and becomes a rubber-necker, staring at plates of food destined for other tables. When her food finally arrives, the sound effects that emerge from her immediately make you wish you had ordered what she has. Then you are forced to hear her detailed, mouthwatering descriptions of her food. You end up wanting to snatch the food off her plate to discover what you are missing! This is the kind of experience we attempt to replicate every time we read with students. We want them to derive the same pleasure and enjoyment from a juicy book that Stephanie can get from a juicy gourmet burger. We want to hear our student's groans when they have to close the book. We want them to be so immersed in text that they are oblivious to what's going on around them. We want them to connect with characters to the extent that when they talk about them, it's as if they are real. We want them to laugh out loud, sigh in worry, and even shed a tear while reading.

Sadly, each and every year we are faced with students who have not experienced the magic of a book. They haven't been captivated by a china rabbit named Edward Tulane (*The Miraculous Journey of Edward Tulane* by Kate DiCamillo); they haven't been troubled by the plight of Ivan trapped in the Big Eight Mall (*The One and Only Ivan* by Katherine Applegate), or been enthralled by the futuristic world of Perses where Christopher and Elena live (*MiNRS* by Kevin Sylvester). For these students the stakes are high. We have to intentionally set up powerful reading experiences that will spark their enthusiasm for reading. We need to change their opinion about what reading holds for them. As teacher–readers, we are perfectly positioned to be that change agent.

Share the Love

Students will
- see and hear from guest readers the pleasure and enjoyment they receive from reading

Calling all readers! It's time to harness the vast reading community that is within your grasp: parents, grandparents, bus drivers, volunteers, before- and after-school caregivers, the variety store owner from down the street, a minister or an imam—you know, someone from the outside. These readers provide the perfect spark to light the flame of reading pleasure and enjoyment.

Daily read-alouds provide the occasion for pleasurable and enjoyable reading moments. Remember, you are not alone in building your community. It's time to call in your local reading allies for support.

1. Spotlight a guest reader on the last day of every month. Ask this individual to keep their visit top secret so a sense of anticipation and excitement can build among your students. Ask your guest to come armed with three texts: their current read, a favorite read, and an age-appropriate read-aloud to share with the class.
2. Ask readers to come prepared to respond to the questions: *Why do you read? In particular what is it that makes reading so pleasurable and enjoyable for you?*
3. Keep a running anchor chart of the reading love your guests share to bear witness to the many ways readers receive pleasure and enjoyment from reading.

Humor: The Heart of Enjoyment

Students will
- be wrapped up in text that leads to giggles, chuckles, and laughter

Did you see the video of Charlie biting his brother's finger? Or the talking twins? What about the baby pandas rolling around at the China zoo? Over the last number of years, our society has been inundated with humorous videos. You can't seem to watch a newscast without a seeing video that leaves you in stitches. Charles Dickens said it best in *A Christmas Carol*: "There is nothing in the world more irresistibly contagious as laughter and good humor." Studies have shown that laughter can decrease stress, reduce anxiety, help you sleep better, burn calories, and release endorphins, while increasing overall happiness. It's essential that our students come to know that one of the reasons that reading is so enjoyable and pleasurable is that it is linked to humor. By intentionally selecting read-alouds that are filled with fun and humor, you send the message to students that reading has a lighter side and that not all texts we explore are serious.

Seek out texts that will lead to full-on belly laughs among your students. Your school librarian can point you in the direction of reputable authors whose books overflow with humor. Our go-to authors include Mélanie Watt, Robert Munsch, Mo Willems, Shel Silverstein, and Roald Dahl.

For older students, consider using *Guys Read Funny Business* edited by Jon Scieszka or *Chicken Soup for the Kids Soul: 101 Stories of Courage, Hope and Laughter* by Jack Canfield and Mark Victor Hansen. These short stories will have your students rolling in laughter and appreciating that one of the main reasons we read is for pleasure and enjoyment.

Reading to Learn

You probably remember the book *All I Really Need to Know I Learned in Kindergarten* by Robert Fulghum. We believe that all you really need to know you can learn from a book! Increasing student background knowledge about a variety of topics, issues, and events can be accomplished with the right piece of text. Want to examine the dangerous journey Syrian refugees take to safety? Read *Stepping Stones* by Margriet Ruurs. Interested in learning more about bees? Read *What's the Buzz? Keeping Bees in Flight* by Merrie-Ellen Wilcox. Curious about the impact of reintroducing a species to an ecosystem? Read *The Wolves Return: A New Beginning for Yellowstone* by Celia Godkin. Or maybe you want to take your students back in time to investigate key historical events. By reading *SIT-IN: How Four Friends Stood Up by Sitting Down* by Andrea Davis Pinkney, your students will discover how a peaceful protest was part of the civil rights movement in the 1960s. Whatever the topic, issue, or event, there's a book for it. These books provide win–win situations.

While students are immersed and swept away by these quality texts it is vital that we draw their attention to the benefits of the read, in particular their increased background knowledge. They may ask, "Why is this important?" The answer: *Because the more you know, the smarter you are.*

Reading-in-the-Real-World Interview

Students will
- interview a parent or guardian to uncover the purposeful reading they do related to their work

> *Anne*
>
> From my first year teaching at a rural school, I remember in particular a student who was quite averse to reading. Peter declared daily that he didn't need to read because he was going to be a farmer. Little did he know that I was born and raised on a farm, and that my secret weapon was my dad. I was still living at home at the time and over dinner I chatted with Dad about all the different reading requirements he has as a farmer; the list was varied and long. Armed with farm equipment manuals, the *Ontario Farmer* newspaper, Chemical Regulation test materials, seed reports, the *Farmer's Almanac*, and more, I returned to school the next day. I set out to address Peter's misconception that farmers were not required to read. After spreading out all my resources and making my case, Peter was convinced that he had some work to do to be farmer, since reading was clearly a requirement.

I wonder if students are aware that each and every job that exists has reading demands. Do they have misconceptions like Peter's that need to be cleared up? Address these head-on by having students interview a parent, guardian, or relative to uncover the reading requirements of their chosen profession. No need to make this a formal or labor-intensive activity; simply have students record the guiding question in their planner (*Can you tell me about the types of reading you need to do for your job?*) and provide each student a lined sticky note to record their findings. The next day, have students share the results of their interview in small groups. Be sure to highlight the vast array of jobs held by interviewees and that all jobs required them to be a proficient reader.

Extension

Consider inviting various school employees into the classroom to share the reading demands of their job: custodian, secretary, speech pathologist, occupational therapist, facility services workers, etc. Or consider having community members come in to your classroom to share.

List the Learning

Students will
- document the new information and understanding they acquire from reading a text

1. For this read-aloud, be explicit that the purpose of the read is to recognize the vast amount of information and understandings we will gain from a particular text:

    Today I am excited to share with you an excerpt from the book, Off to Class: Incredible and Unusual Schools Around the World *by Susan Hughes. While I read aloud I am going to ask you to track and document all the information that is new to you. At the end I will be asking you to share your new knowledge with your classmates.*

2. When reading, keep in mind that the knowledge students gain will be both right-there, put-your-finger-on-it knowledge and enduring understandings of the big ideas that cannot be found directly on the page.
3. After reading, record a piece of new background knowledge from each student. Be sure to acknowledge the student by name beside the nugget of knowledge. If more than one student has the same nugget, record both names.
4. Sum up by exclaiming, "The more you read the more you know. And aren't we lucky to have access to so many books!"

Becoming a News Hound

Students will
- investigate various websites to build their background knowledge on a weekly basis

Nelson Mandela stated, "An educated, enlightened and informed population is one of the surest ways of promoting the health of a democracy" (Mandela, 2003). As teachers, we need to steal moments from our busy curriculum to inform young minds about events and situations currently facing our world. We are fortunate that many age-appropriate websites are just a click away. The following sites let our students access timely and informative content: Wonderopolis, DOGO News, Time For Kids, Teaching Kids News, Scholastic News, and PBS NEWSHOUR EXTRA (Grades 7–12). Or you might check out Currents4Kids (Grades 3 and up) and What in the World? from Lesplan Educational Services. Each of these sources provides an abundance of news on a variety of subjects: current events, science, social studies, sports, arts, etc. Infuse your classroom with news, tapping into your students' innate curiosities to know more about their world. At first, you will need to sniff out the news, draw students' attention to these websites, and provide the time and space to share these articles in class. But before long your students' insatiable desire to know more about their world will compel them to seek out the news on their own; all you need to provide is the time, access, and validation. To clearly communicate the value and importance of being an informed citizen, sharing and discussing current news events must happen on a weekly basis. As news stories are shared, use these prompts: What new information have we added to our background knowledge? Why is it important that we know about this?

Reading to Become Better Writers

Imitation is the highest form of flattery. As the lead readers in the classroom, we set out each day to perform at a high standard in terms of oral reading. We intend for students to emulate this "reader voice" in their own heads when they read independently and when they read aloud. The same is true for writing. We want students to emulate phenomenal writers. Since we can't physically bring an actual writer into the room each day, we do the next best thing by bringing authors' art into the room in the form of their books. Just as we have modeled exemplary reading to students, we set out to do the same with excellent writing. We highlight quality text for students to use as mentors for their own writing.

Based on his meta-analysis of reading research, Steven Krashen informs us that "writing style does not come from actual writing experience, but from

If you are interested in learning about the power of mentor text to elevate student writing, we recommend Lynne Dorfman and Rose Cappelli's *Mentor Text Series* as well as *Crafting Writers* by Elizabeth Hale, and *Marvelous Minilessons* by Lori Jamison Rog.

reading" (Krashen, 2004, p. 132). So let's ensure that our students are reading text that is chock full of writing potential. According to Dorfman and Cappelli, "A mentor text is a book that offers myriad possibilities for our students and for ourselves as writers" (Dorfman and Cappelli, 2007 p. 3). Mentor texts can stimulate ideas, introduce new writing formats, offer unique text structures, model craft techniques, present distinctive word choice, and ignite a passion for writers to mine their own lives for writing possibilities. It's time to open the eyes and ears of our readers, for them to see and hear the beauty of the written word. When we find ourselves moved by text during a read-aloud we must stop and savor the moment with our students. Let them hear you "Oooh" and "Aaah" over stunning language. Our reaction to writing models shows our students the value we place on the author's words to touch and move our hearts, minds, and hands. Don't let the words rush over you quickly like a waterfall; instead, slow your reading down and relish the moment.

Stories that Spark Writing

Students will
- use text being read aloud as a stimulus for their own writing ideas

Stories trigger memories. They draw us in and compel us to reminisce about our own personal experiences. The story connects the writer and reader in a profound and intimate way. As teachers, we can stage these opportunities by selecting text that will stimulate connection and recollection, books that inspire students to write in the style and pattern of the author and serve as fodder for personal writing ideas. Inspect your classroom collection or the library to find titles that can be used as a springboard for student writing.

1. Choose a section of text to use as a mentor text for writing about memories:

> When I was young in the mountains,
> Grandfather came home in the evening covered with the black dust of a coal mine.
> Only his lips were clean, and he used them to kiss the top of my head.
> —from *When I Was Young in the Mountains* by Cynthia Rylant

After you have read aloud the text, encourage students to reflect on a place that holds a special place in their heart; for example, a cottage or campground, a park or conservation area, homes of relatives or friends, the local hockey arena or community centre. Ask them to write a few significant memories associated with that particular place.

Student sample: Luke, Grade 6

> When I was young in Lambeth I loved to go hiking in the forest behind my Grandparents house with them and my brother and sister. We never had a particular destination in mind, we would just turn around whenever we were tired. My favorite hikes took place in winter on cold crisp days when there was a blanket of snow on the ground. I loved seeing the animal tracks in the snow. We would hike around fallen trees, over old farm fences, and through tall grass. My grandpa would bring his special hockey stick without the blade in case of coyotes. When we returned to the warm house if you were lucky we were able to sneak my grandma's amazing chocolate chip peanut butter balls into your mouth.

2. Choose a text that inspires students to reflect on the impact the unique features of the region in which they live has on their daily lives:

If you're not from the prairie,
You don't know the sun,
You can't know the sun.
Diamonds that bounce off crisp winter snows
Warm water in dugouts and lakes that we know.
The sun is our friend from when we are young,
A child of the prairie is part of the sun.
If you're not from the prairie,
You don't know the sun.
— from *If You're Not from the Prairie* by David Bouchard

Students can write about harsh winters, high winds, humid summers, or ice in the harbor. Or they can turn it into a unique piece about their school or family.

Student sample: Cooper, Grade 6

If you're not from the Kelly family
You don't know cat hair.
You can't know cat hair.
The grey magnetic black fabric-seeking hair will do you no harm
But it will cling to almost anything you don't want it to.
Wherever you travel it is always there to remind you of who you left at home.
If you're not from the Kelly family
You don't know cat hair.

Another good text for this is *The Matchbox Diary* by Paul Fleischman.

3. Choose a text about artifacts that have meaning:

He looked for the shoe-box of shells he had found long ago last summer, and put them gently in a basket. He found the puppet strings which always made everyone laugh and he put that in the basket too. He remembered with sadness the medal which his grandfather had given him and he placed it gently next to the shells.
— from *Wilfrid Gordon MacDonald Partridge* by Mem Fox

After reading this text aloud, students seek out their own artifacts that hold significant memories for them and use them as an impetus for their own writing.

Replicating our Favorite Writers

Students will
- understand the connection between reading and writing, and learn to listen as a writer to gather craft

When our purpose for a read-aloud is to influence and inspire our young writers, we need to intentionally select texts that fit the bill. As the lead reader in the classroom, we must draw students' attention to writer's craft techniques found in quality text; however, not during the first read—that is for pure enjoyment. Most young readers and writers don't notice the craft techniques authors use to communicate vividly to their readers, and there was a time when we didn't either. It's not a lack of ability to identify these techniques, rather a lack of experience in doing so. It is our job to slow down the reading to share our excitement and enthusiasm for beautiful writing. We must revisit powerful parts that demand a second read. As well, we must name and label these specific craft techniques that writers use. That way we enable our students to recognize these techniques in their independent reading; once this happens, they are empowered to read with a writer's eyes. In our experience, once students are aware of specific craft techniques such as alliteration, simile, magic of three, proper nouns/brand names, etc., there is no stopping them.

Samples are from the one book that stands out for both of us in terms of stunning language, expertly used craft techniques, and captivating message: *Saturdays and Teacakes* by Lester Laminack.

Samples of The Magic of Three

Every Saturday I got up early, dressed, and rolled my bicycle out of the garage.

Every Saturday she had hot biscuits, sweet butter, and Golden Eagle Syrup waiting on the kitchen table.

Samples of Repetition

Pedal, pedal, pedal, past Mrs. Cofield's house. Pedal, pedal, pedal, around the horse pasture and up the hill past the cemetery where my grandfather was buried. Pedal, pedal, pedal, past Mrs. Grace Owen's house and on up to Chandler's Phillips 66.

Every Saturday...

Samples of Onomatopoeia

Whoosh!
criiick-craaack-criiick-craaack

Samples of Metaphor

Just before reaching Mammaw's back porch, I slammed on my brakes, sending a shower of tiny pebbles into her flowers.

Every Saturday she spread a cloth over the red countertop and scattered a fistful of flour across it, sending a cloud into the air.

Samples of Simile

In Mammaw's big kitchen, sunlight poured through the window like a waterfall and spilled over the countertops, pooling up on the checkerboard floor.

Every Saturday I gobbled mine down like a hungry dog, but she nibbled at hers like a bird.

Samples of Alliteration

Every Saturday I pulled the starter rope again and again while the mower sputtered and spit.

I mixed and mashed and mixed and mashed until the ingredients disappeared into a paste.

Samples of Using Proper Nouns/Brand Names

Blue Bonnet
Frigidaire

Sample of Vivid Verbs

We encourage you to keep an anchor chart of all these techniques entitled Writer's Craft Techniques.

> Mammaw dipped a china teacup into the canister of flour, scooped out a cupful, and skimmed over the top with her finger. Then she dumped the flour into the bowl and added sugar from her black cookie jar.

Reading to Build Vocabulary

The more you exercise, the more strength and stamina you develop. The more strength and stamina you develop, the more strenuous and difficult exercises you are able to do. The same can be said for building an advanced vocabulary. Kelly Gallagher states, "The more you read, the more new words you encounter. The more new words you encounter, the more new words you learn" (Gallagher, 2003, p. 52). Students need us to connect being a reader with developing a broader vocabulary.

Research clearly demonstrates the importance of vocabulary to students' literacy success. The development of vocabulary has been shown to promote reading fluency, boost reading comprehension, improve academic achievement, and enhance thinking and communication (Bromley, 2004). When our students read daily, we are giving them a vocabulary booster shot—reading in itself will improve their vocabulary. In addition, let's provide our students with a little extra medicine—explicit instruction. We recommend deliberately reading aloud text that elevates student vocabulary and crafting activities that support students in understanding the importance of context in obtaining meaning from unfamiliar vocabulary.

Newfangled and Novel Words

Students will
- use read-aloud text as a stimulus for acquiring new vocabulary in context

Increasing student vocabulary can be done with any book, at any time, anywhere. You would be hard pressed to find a text that doesn't have a few new words for students to add to their ever-growing vocabulary bank. But let's not leave the learning of these words to chance: spotlight these unfamiliar words and decipher their meaning from the context in which they appear.

You have to model interrupting the reading to untangle the meaning of new vocabulary. When you pretend to not know particular words in a read-aloud, you will without a doubt have a student eager to tell you what the word means. But try to ignore them and commit to modeling how to use context clues to help the rest of the class decipher the meaning of the unknown word. Do not rely on the talking dictionary in the class to define words—students need to learn how to use context clues to assist them in inferring the meaning of unknown words.

If you want a fun vocabulary workout for middle-grade students, investigate Margaret Atwood's *Princess Prunella and the Purple Peanut* or *Rude Ramsay and the Roaring Radishes*. For younger audiences, try *Some Smug Slug* or *Dinorella* by Pamela Duncan Edwards. These texts are filled to the brim with alliteration and distinctive word choice that will have your students sweating trying to determine the meaning of new vocabulary.

> In time, her hands became burnt and scarred. Her arms too became rough and scarred. Even her face was marked by the fire, and her beautiful long black hair hung ragged and charred.
> — from *The Rough-Face Girl* by Rafe Martin

Your lesson might sound like this:

Let me read that part again because there were a couple of words in that paragraph that I didn't know: ragged *and* charred. *I'm not sure what those words mean. I think*

I should read the entire paragraph again and see if other words in that section give me some clues as to what they mean. I know that her hands and arms are burnt and scarred and that she is by a fire. I know that when something is burnt it becomes blackened, so I'm thinking that the word charred *is another way of saying that something is burned and blackened by fire. I also know that when hair gets burnt it becomes frizzy and shrivels up, so I'm thinking that the word* ragged *describes how uneven her hair looks after being burned.*

Elevate Your Vocabulary

Students will
- use read-aloud text as a stimulus for acquiring new vocabulary in context and identifying synonyms and antonyms

To create a vocabulary-rich environment, consider creating a cumulative vocabulary word wall in your classroom. Simply use unfamiliar words encountered in your read-aloud and shared-reading texts.

1. Model a variety of strategies for seeking out the meaning of unfamiliar words. Sometimes the context in which the word appears provides clues and allow us to infer the meaning. Other times we need to analyze the parts of the word or solicit the assistance of the dictionary or thesaurus. Using one or more of these methods, figure out the meaning of the word, based on the context in which it is used.
2. Print the words onto large cards and display in a prominent place. To expand the definition, add synonyms in smaller font under each word. Try to have five to seven words on this list at a time.
3. To promote independent student use of the word, add a tally mark beside the word each time a student employs it correctly in a lesson (Ontario Literacy and Numeracy Secretariat). You will be surprised how the incentive of tally marks increases student attention to the words.
4. Once a word has been used at least ten times, retire it to your vocabulary word wall. Revisit retired words by doing the following:
   - ask students to define the meaning of a word selected from the wall
   - provide a definition of a word and ask students to identify the word
   - identify a synonym for one of the words on the wall and challenge students to find its match

Picture Books That Inspire Word Detectives

The Word Collector by Sonja Amato
Max's Words by Kate Banks
Wonderful Words selected by Lee Bennett Hopkins
The Boy Who Cried Fabulous by Leslea Newman
The Boy Who Loved Words by Roni Schotter
The Very Inappropriate Word by Jim Tobin

Reading to Learn Life Lessons

In *Leah's Pony* by Elizabeth Friedrich, Leah teaches her community about the meaning of sacrifice and selflessness when she is willing to sell her prized pony to buy back her father's tractor at the auction. In *Each Kindness* by Jacqueline Woodson, when Maya abruptly moves before Chloe can make amends, Chloe learns that you don't always get a second chance to do the right thing. In *The Junkyard Wonders* by Patricia Polacco, Mrs. Peterson imparts to her students that each and every one of them is more than a label and that they have remarkable gifts inside them just waiting to blossom. In *Ish* by Peter Reynolds, Marisol teaches Ramon that not everything needs to be perfect; sometimes things can be *ish*. In *Mr. Peabody's Apples* by Madonna, Mr. Peabody instills in Billy Little the life lesson that his words have power and that there is danger in spreading rumors.

Books are in the lesson business. Between the pages of every text, an author leaves the reader priceless gifts—big ideas, life lessons, morals—just waiting to be discovered. Stories with memorable characters provide wisdom and insight into situations and events that our students may or may not experience first-hand. Reading enables us to peek through the window into another life, look into a mirror and see ourselves, and open doors to other worlds. Living vicariously through characters, we are able to explore serious and sensitive topics, such as poverty, divorce, death, bullying, discrimination, disability, and racism. Books afford the reader an opportunity to learn, to grow, and to be changed. Shelley Stagg Peterson and Larry Swartz affirm what we know as teachers: "Literature gives students vicarious experiences and helps them live more lives than the ones they think they have" (Peterson and Swartz, 2008, p. 9).

What's the Secret Message?

Students will
- identify the big idea or life lesson they take from a read-aloud

It's essential that we create the conditions for students to reflect on text and consider the life lessons and big ideas hidden within stories. These kernels of wisdom are waiting for the reader to discover and relate to their own lives. We long for students to finish text so they can think about and ponder the following questions: *What have you learned from this story? What has the character taught you? What lessons will stay with you? What message(s) was the author covertly sending you?*

1. Introduce this activity by saying

   Did you know that the author of today's story sent us a secret life lesson? We will not find this lesson explicitly on the page. We won't be able to put our finger on it, rather we will have to infer the secret message from events in the story and the characters' actions. We may have to piece it together from beginning to end.

2. Following the read-aloud, have students discuss in small groups what they believe or think the secret message might be. Distribute slips of paper to each student and have them commit their secret message to writing. For example, after a read-aloud of *A Bike Like Sergio's* by Maribeth Boelts, students were captivated by Ruben's struggle to do the right thing after finding one hundred dollars at the grocery store. In small groups they generated the following lessons:

   - Doing the right thing is sometimes hard.
   - You don't always get a reward for doing what is right.
   - It's never wrong to do the right thing.
   - Not telling the truth can make you feel sick inside.

3. Collect the slips and begin as a class to sort them thematically, noting similarities and trends among student ideas.

4. Consolidate student thinking by drafting an all-encompassing secret message that merges and validates the thinking of the class. For example, the secret message we generated from the book *A Bike Like Sergios* was this: *Making the right choice isn't always easy. It might not immediately feel better in your head but it will in your heart.*

Recording student thinking validates and honors student voice.

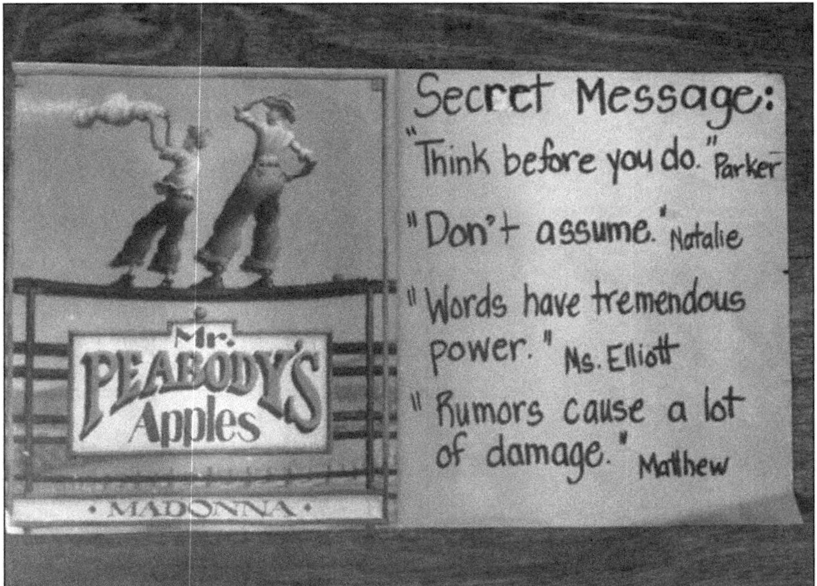

5. Put the drafted secret message into an envelope that has been tacked into the back of the book.

Extension

Consider placing the text, as well as others you investigate, in a special bin for students to reread and rediscover the class message. Sensational learning takes place when students reread the text with new eyes and discover a different lesson to add to the envelope. The message they independently generate will be imprinted on their mind and heart. Be sure to periodically revisit this lesson with a new title to continue reinforcing that we read to learn valuable life lessons.

Big Idea Bank

Students will
- co-construct an ongoing anchor chart of big ideas or life lessons they take from read-alouds

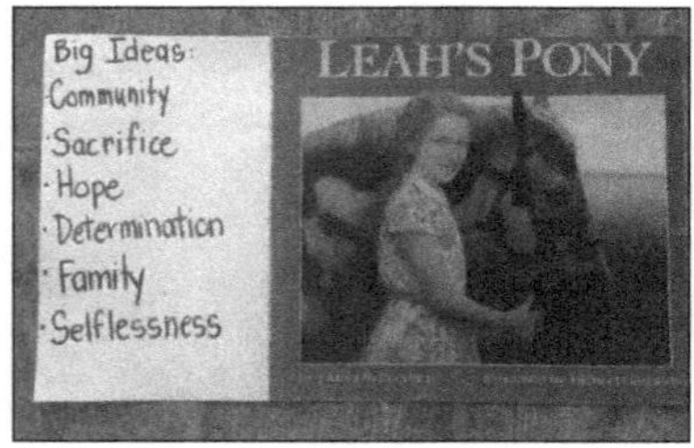

Our dear friends Annette Gilbert and Jane Baird contend that there is not an infinite number of big ideas to be found in text. Rather, key themes return again and again in books for us to contemplate and internalize, big ideas like perseverance, honesty, kindness, determination, generosity, selflessness, the importance of community, and being a steward of the earth. It is the thinking and the talking we do around these big ideas that cements and fortifies their connection to our lives.

A powerful practice is to create a visible record of this thinking in the form of a co-constructed anchor chart. This enables us to hold on to our thinking and allows us to revisit and refer back to it time and again. As the bank grows over time, draw students' attention to the connection between characters, their experiences, and their actions, and the lessons learned. Following a read-aloud, have students consider the following questions: *What have you learned from this story? What has the character taught you? What lessons will stay with you? What message(s) was the author covertly sending you?* Color copy the cover of the book onto a large piece of paper and record student thinking on the remaining white space. Cluster and display these charts prominently in your community gathering area to anchor conversation about big ideas in text.

Books that Make you Move

Books have the power to call us to think, talk, and act differently in our world. You cannot read the picture book *Stepping Stones* by Margriet Ruurs without thinking about the blessings of your life compared to the plight of Rama and her family as they escape war-torn Syria as refugees. You cannot read an article about the detrimental impact of microbeads on our ecosystems without starting to question what you purchase and considering changing your habits. You cannot read the picture books *When I Was Eight* and *Not My Girl* by Christy Jordan-Fenton and Margaret Pokiak-Fenton without being moved to tears by Olemaun's experience in a residential school and the devastating impact it has on her and her family. You cannot read the novel *A Long Walk to Water* by Linda Sue Park without reflecting on the impact access to clean water has on some children's lives in Africa.

After reading these texts, our awareness of the issues within the pages is heightened. We are compelled to talk to others and share our new knowledge. All of a sudden, our eyes and ears are open to these issues and we begin to see connections between text and the real world. We see it on the front page of newspapers, in magazines, and on news updates on Internet browsers. We hear it on radio broadcasts and see it on the nightly news.

We might also see it on billboards and signs in our local communities. For example, after Mary's class read the Scholastic article "Shattered Lives" and the online article "What they Carried," students became very concerned about the refugee crisis. Learning that refugees are forced to leave most of their belongings behind, they were deeply touched. They began to care about this issue and sought out additional information on their own. When they found out that Merrymount, a local organization, was collecting toys for refugee children who had settled in the community, they were eager to offer support. A schoolwide toy drive for refugees was born. Announcements, posters, and flyers sent home spoke to their knowledge, passion, and commitment. The overwhelming response from the community made it clear to students that they could make a real difference in the world. Such reading experiences can be seeds to our students becoming change agents.

Turning the Tables

As teachers we expect our students to take us at our word that reading is valuable and important, simply because we say so. We admit that too often we have fallen into the role as the primary reading motivator by handing out stickers, ribbons, pins, certificates, pencils, erasers, pizza—you name it, we supplied it! But we know that to intrinsically motivate students to be lifelong readers we must move beyond cheap tricks. We want our students to recognize that reading is its own reward. The activities described throughout this chapter show your students the many benefits of reading. Now it's time to ask your students to answer the vital question: *Why read?* Be prepared to be astounded by the countless reasons they come up with. Gather their thinking on a Why Read anchor chart and prominently display it in the classroom for all to see. As more reading reasons are discovered, add them to the chart.

Anne's Grade 6 students and Stephanie Cook's Grade 3 students have many reasons to read.

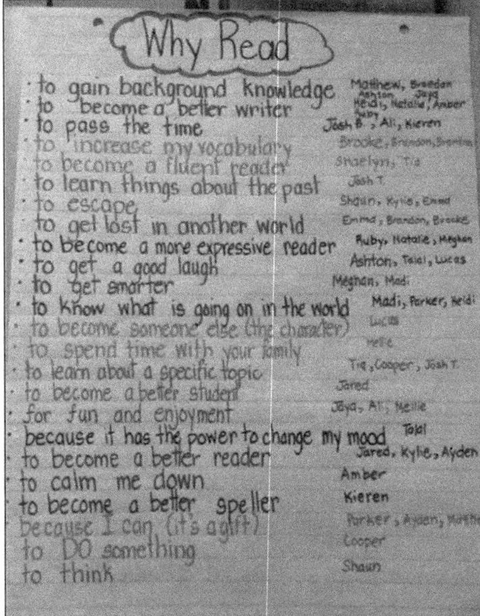

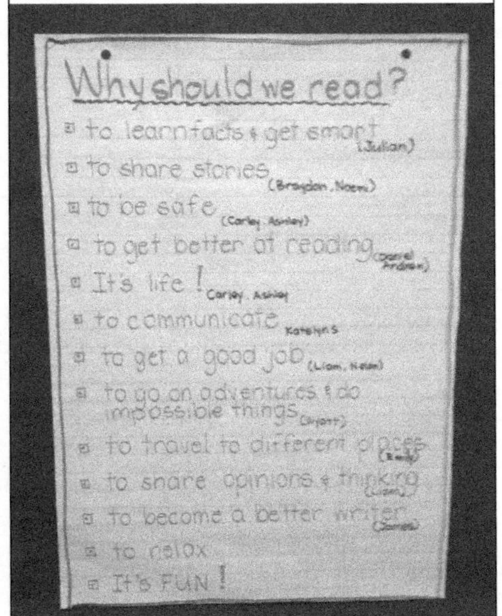

6

Fifth Step: Creating the Space

We have a confession to make: we're addicted to HGTV and home renovation TV shows. We think it's because they take a house, a yard, or a room that seems to be beyond repair, and within a short period of time they transform it into something you would expect to see in a magazine, a space that is organized, beautiful, stylish, and, above all, inviting. Our favorite moment is always the big reveal, when the owners arrive home full of anticipation and nervousness. The interior designer or contractor milks the moment by reviewing the owners' previous discontent with the space and their long wish list for improvement. And then the moment is upon us, drum roll please... no bathroom breaks now!

As viewers we get caught up in the moment and share the owner's excitement and sense of joy when they see their transformed space for the first time. And before you know it our heads are filled with our own renovation dreams and possibilities. We start looking around our homes and envisioning new paint colors, different flooring and accent pieces. They make it look easy to refurbish old furniture purchased for next to nothing at the local thrift store and to rearrange pieces to magically change a space. This is not a task we do that often in our homes (much to the relief of our bank accounts) but we do renovate a space each and every year, and sometimes even throughout the year—our classrooms, the space where we spend more time in than in our homes!

As self-confessed HGTV addicts, we have been bitten by the outdoor living design bug that has been buzzing around the last few years. We have the outdoor furniture, rugs, lighting, and décor to prove it. But purchasing the materials occurred after thoughtful design that took into account what we wanted to do in this space. We wanted shaded spaces and sunny places. We longed to sit, escape the noise, and listen to the sounds of nature; at other times we wanted to gather together with family and friends and while away an afternoon. We wanted a space to relax and lounge with a good book, a spot to play and laugh with friends, and even a place to cook and eat. Not to mention a fire pit for roasting marshmallows late at night.

Is classroom design and set-up really any different from setting up your backyard oasis? When someone visits your classroom, adult or student, would they know that this environment is home to a reading community? Would the physical design and layout of the space clearly communicate that this is a place where readers live? As teachers we must take into account what we want to do in our reading classrooms. Our priorities are

- a large gathering area that will seat the entire class
- a small-group meeting area for conferences, book clubs, and focused instruction
- various nooks around the room where students can curl up and read
- a space for a diverse and abundant classroom library
- multiple spaces for book displays

And don't forget the attractive décor—plants, cushions, and lamps.

Stay with us. I know what you're thinking: *Have you seen the size of my room? Do you know how many students I have? Do you know how big the desks are?* We face the same challenges when arranging our classrooms. But we have to be creative and work with what we've got! Building the physical space for our reading community takes intention and ingenuity. So let's investigate the rationale for each component.

Reading by the Numbers

Gathering the Whole Class

> *Anne*
>
> Last weekend my family went to the horse races at Woodbine Racetrack in Toronto. During the two-hour drive from London, I was excited about getting there and being able to interact, visit, and chit-chat with everyone. I envisioned all of us sitting around a huge round table, being able to connect with one another. Unfortunately, as soon as we were seated it was apparent that this was going to be a challenge, as we were spread out at three different rectangular tables, so my conversation was limited to whoever was directly across and beside me. We did interact as small groups but not as a family, and I left with the feeling that I missed out on a lot of stories, conversations, and fun.

The large gathering area serves to nourish and support our steadily growing reading community and our interconnectedness to one another.

When our students are seated around the room and are asked to interact with a neighbor, they are limited to conversing with those who are in close proximity to them. And sometimes this is suitable and sufficient. On the other hand, when our intention is to engage as a reading community, desks and tables are no longer the place to be! It is time to draw the gang together in a large gathering area, preferably carpeted for comfort. Having a close communal area is a non-negotiable for us, as it is the location that unifies and cements us as a community of readers. Think for a moment of sports teams: the home of the Toronto Blue Jays is the Rogers Centre, the Toronto Maple Leafs live at the Air Canada Centre, the Boston Red Sox reside at Fenway Park, and the Dallas Cowboys inhabit AT&T Stadium. Every team, squad, club has a space that unites and bonds them. The large gathering area in your room becomes the home of your reading community. The ritual of coming together in this defined space is symbolic. When you are performing read-alouds and shared reading, having your students physically gathered close as one group is vital because proximity matters.

Proximity to the Text

We want our students to actively engage and interact with what we are reading to and with them. For example, when we are reading a picture book, students must be near enough to see the powerful illustrations that serve to elevate the story. During shared reading, whether using a big book or screen, students must be able to clearly read the passage.

Proximity to the Teacher

Conducting a read-aloud is a performance, and there is nothing like a front-row seat at a show. We all want to see the entertainer's face. When they are close to us physically, students benefit from seeing the subtle changes on our faces that communicate emotion and meaning. As we alter our voices from a whisper to a shout, students are mesmerized and enthralled by the story. Proximity is a factor in achieving this experience. If we want to be able to look right into our students' eyes, to hook their minds, and touch their hearts, then we must be close enough to draw them in.

Proximity to One Another

The authentic conversation that occurs during and after reading benefits from proximity as well. The ability to express our thoughts and perspectives and build on the thinking of one another is supported by physical closeness. In particular, sitting in a circle enables eye contact to be made with the speaker by everyone in the group, conveying respect. It also increases student engagement in the conversation and facilitates dialogue among the community. This can lead to the creation of shared understandings of the text and an awareness of different perspectives.

Small Groups Unite

Just as there is power in the entire classroom reading community coming together to interact with text, a case can be made for having a space in our classrooms for small groups to congregate. Whether you gather on the floor on comfy pillows or cluster chairs around a small table or a guided-reading horseshoe, the fact is that you need a space to sit eye-to-eye, to lean in, and to chat with one another about your reading. The purpose of a small-group meeting area is to provide an intimate location away from the bustle of the class to meet for focused instruction, reading conferences, and book clubs. Space for small groups to collaborate and communicate are essential to a reading community.

A Nook for One

> *Mary*
>
> I don't choose to read at the kitchen table. I don't like to sit in my home office and read a novel. I don't enjoy reading in a room with the TV on or with people talking near me. But I do choose to read in the den on my recliner. I love to read on my bed propped up on pillows. I enjoy reading in the hammock under a shady tree.

When given the choice, readers seek out spaces and places to read that are comfortable and quiet. In *The Power of Reading,* Steven Krashen states that the physical characteristics of the reading environment are important. This is what Morrow discovered when examining the library in Kindergarten classrooms. He found that when the library "had pillows, easy chairs, and carpets, and when it was partitioned off and quiet" (Morrow, 1983/Krashen, 2004), it was used more often. We believe that all readers crave comfort and quiet no matter their age. So if we provide precious time for students to immerse themselves in reading, why would we not provide them with an ideal environment?

Where are the comfy, cozy, quiet places in your room for students to curl up and read? When arranging your classroom furniture, mindfully create little nooks around the room where students can get comfortable, and be alone with a book. We want them to be able to read like readers in their natural habitat. So hit the shops, thrift stores, and garden centres in search of practical chairs, coffee tables, rugs, and décor. Summer is the perfect time to purchase affordable, kid-friendly furniture. We have had great luck with outdoor lawn chairs in a variety of colors, sizes, and designs. As well, consider plastic Adirondack chairs, beach chairs, beanbags, oversized pillows, and carpet squares. These attractive reading spaces offer an alternative to the formal chair and desk. They add to the reading ambiance in the room and replicate real reading places outside the classroom. Reading nooks communicate to everyone that comfy, cozy, and quiet reading happens in this room.

Waiting for readers

Lost in a book

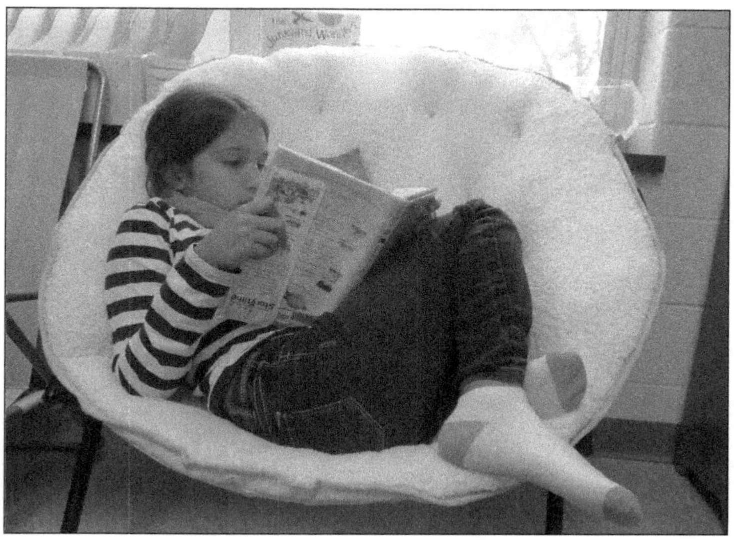

The Classroom Library

You can't be a hair stylist without scissors. You can't be a photographer without a camera. You can't be a chef without a set of knives. You can't be a reading teacher if you don't have a classroom library. You can't cultivate a reader without books. Every profession has tools, and ours are books! Lots and lots of books and magazines are the currency on which our community grows, thrives, and flourishes. Literacy guru Regie Routman argues

> the availability of reading materials greatly impacts children's literacy development. The most effective reading programs are generally supported by large classroom libraries. The better the libraries, the better the reading achievement as measured by standardized tests. (Routman, 2003)

So what are you waiting for? Start building a mini book store in your classroom.

You might be thinking: "We have an outstanding school library that we visit every cycle. Why do I need my own library?" Because that one library visit every cycle is not enough to cultivate a reader. You want to create an environment in which students are surrounded by text so that books are always accessible. A classroom library is never closed. Its hours of operation are from the time the bell rings to the time everyone goes home.

In the video *Building Adolescent Readers* (2004) Kelly Gallagher shares an anecdote that illustrates the importance of proximity to text. He tells the story of conducting a book talk with his class and detailing the exact route students need to take to reach the school library where the book is located. He immediately laments the fact that, when the bell rings, students scatter and move on to the next class, and the book is quickly forgotten. Conversely when he sells his class on the same book, this time with the text in hand, he has readers eagerly reaching for it and is forced to create a waiting list. That book is gone and he doesn't see it until the end of the year. Proximity to text matters.

Knowing Your Collection

Our Board aims to have school library collections that comprise 20–25 items per student. For example, in a school of 500 there would be approximately 12,500 items. It is completely unrealistic to think that a classroom teacher would personally know the school collection so well to easily match texts to students. I'm sure you would agree that it is more manageable for teachers to know the books in their classroom libraries. Intimately knowing your classroom library collection allows you to readily match texts to readers. You're able to quickly respond to students' specific requests, to suggest alternatives, and to make recommendations. Knowing the collection allows you to identify what is there, what is not there, and what gaps exist between your collection and students' needs and interests.

Stephanie Cook's inviting classroom library

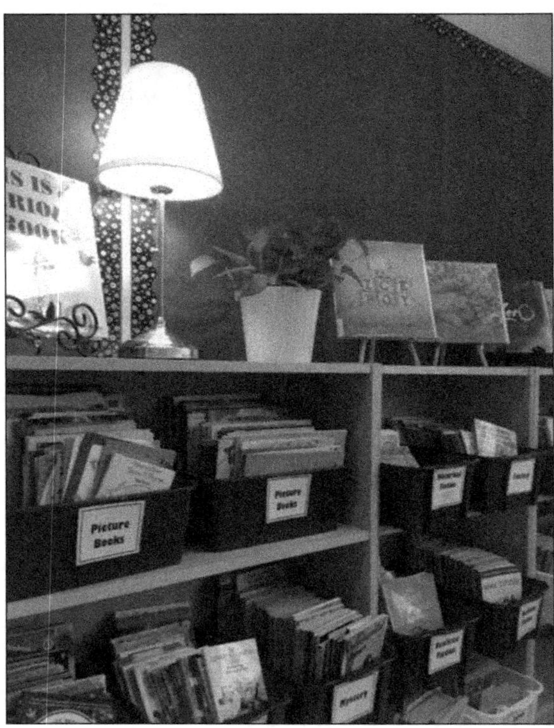

Customizing Your Collection

Not only are our classroom libraries much smaller in size, they are also carefully customized to the match the age, maturity, reading ability, and interests of our students. Moreover, we augment the collection with text tied to curriculum. Because the school library must meet the vast needs of all grades, it can be overwhelming to students and difficult to navigate. Have you ever observed students searching for their next read in the school library? We call it the lean-and-look pose. Students hinge over at the waist and crane their necks to read the spine of each book. What an ineffective and uncomfortable way to peruse the stacks for their next read! Not to mention the fact that they miss out on the cover. Consider how Chapters and Indigo entice you from the moment you enter: display tables covered with a bounty of books face up, captivating covers clearly on display. In our classroom libraries we have complete control over how books are displayed and featured. We can choose which authors, series, genres, and even text sets to spotlight in a variety of creative ways. As well, in our classroom libraries we are not confined by the three traditional organizational categories of school libraries: Nonfiction, Fiction and Picture Books. With our students we can decide an organization for the books that best meets their needs and literary understanding. For example, in Grade 3 you might have a bin labeled *Scary Stories*, whereas in Grade 7 you might call it *Horror*, *Thrillers*, or *Murder Mysteries*. You might even have all three. When you honor student input, you increase their ownership of the classroom collection. It is most effective to ensure that books are displayed in bins that allow them to be upright, cover out, so students can flip through and allow their eye to be lured by the titles and covers.

Reading Your Collection

Last, but certainly not least, your classroom library is well-read by you, the reading teacher. We cannot stress enough the power, influence, and ability you hold as the lead reader in the room when you can speak authentically about books you've read from your collection. When Mya returned the book *Rain Reign* by Ann M. Martin to Ms. Elliott, she emphatically disclosed that it was the best book she ever read and was moved to tears. Because Ms. Elliott had also been swept away by that story, she was able to engage in a real reader conversation with Mya. Together they spoke of Rose's heartbreaking decision, her discovery about her mother, and the life-altering ending of the book. Ms. Elliott and Mya connected head-to-head, heart-to-heart, reader-to-reader! You can't fake this. It is imperative that we, as reading teachers, read as many of the books in our collection as possible. This allows us to genuinely book talk titles, to reliably link specific readers with books that will be smash hits, and to have sincere reader conversations with students. Together these actions cultivate the will to read. Our goal is for our readers to enjoy many more hits than misses, so that they will come to know that our classroom library is a gold mine filled with treasures. There is no escaping the value of a classroom library. It is essential.

Appraising Your Classroom Library

In our system, school librarians are required to critically examine their collection each year. Similarly we need to scrutinize our classroom libraries annually. Use the following questions as a guide:

- Would you categorize your library as current and fresh or dated and tired?
- Would you say your library is abundant? Solid? Or limited? Do you believe your students have plenty of choice?
- Does your library contain various genres and forms? Fiction: realistic, historical, fantasy, mystery, adventure, humor? Nonfiction: biography, autobiography, memoir, earth and space, people and places, animals? What about poetry?
- Can students access classics, tried-and-true authors, and shiny, new titles in your library?
- Will students be able to easily locate favorite authors and series in the library?
- Does your library accommodate a range of reading abilities?
- Will students find lighter gateway text in the collection, books that provide them an entry point into reading as they develop their stamina and love of quality literature?

- Is your library inclusive? Does it promote a sense of belonging? Will your students see themselves reflected in the text in your library? Does it honor the diversity of your classroom, larger community, and greater world?
- Will your classroom library support students in gaining background knowledge related to your grade curriculum?
- Do you routinely add to the collection throughout the school year as interests and preferences emerge and change? As students grow as readers, do you change the books?

Vast and Varied

If the rule of thumb for the number of items a school library should have in its collection per student is 20-25, we can cut that benchmark in half and arrive at 10–12 items per student for classroom libraries. That is, in a class of 25 we would need approximately 250 items to support our readers. Think of that amount as a starting point for an acceptable library. Bins and baskets should never be empty or appear sparse after students have book shopped; rather, their abundance should communicate endless choice to readers. We know that reader choice is directly connected to their will to read. So let's ensure that they have a vast collection to choose from. This collection must also be varied. As we strive for our students to have a balanced reading diet, we must guarantee that our classroom libraries support them in reading from a variety of genres. So make sure your library has it all, suiting the age and reading ability of your readers.

Building a vast and varied library collection takes time and money. We suggest new teachers or someone new to a division consider the following ideas for growing your library:

- In our city we are lucky to have a number of used book stores as well as donation centres that focus on gently used books. Their great selection and affordable prices make it feasible to come away with an amazing stack of engaging titles. However, we strongly suggest being a critical consumer. Stay away from yellow, tattered, or worn books. If they look dated and dirty, students will not pick them up. Let's face it—neither would you.
- In our classrooms we have a book donation bin that encourages students to donate their own gently used books to our classroom library. When cleaning out bedrooms, many parents are quite willing and eager to pass along books to a new home.
- The Scholastic book clubs are a phenomenal source for current and affordable titles. Their bonus points program enables you to take advantage of student sales and use the points earned to augment your collection. Each month, when passing out the book order, we have students highlight two or three titles they wish were part of the classroom library. We collate this information and then use points to make these purchases. Students are elated to know that their choices will soon be in the collection.
- It is not the classroom teacher's sole responsibility to finance the classroom library. Use the power of persuasion (and the information in this book) to make a pitch to your administrator and Home and School Association to financially support your growing classroom library. It takes a whole school community to raise a reader, and each stakeholder must contribute.

Honoring Student Voice

In Chapter 3 we examined the valuable information gathered from student interest and reading surveys. These sources provide you with students' favorite authors, series, particular titles, topics, and genres. It's vital that students see their preferences and interests reflected in the classroom library, since this is the primary source of their reading material. Use this information to guide your purchases for the class. For example, if Stuart Gibbs and Michael Wade are mentioned as favorite authors on surveys or during classroom conversations, then make sure your library contains their books.

Staying Current

Each year new authors and titles emerge that get a tremendous amount of buzz from the literary community. Mr. Schu Reads, the Nerdy Book Club, Amazon, and Twitter light up with cover reveals, trailers, and reviews. Shiny, new titles hold an exclusive appeal to readers. We want to be one of the first people to read that book! As well, purchasing new books in a series fosters reader momentum. To create added anticipation and buzz around an upcoming title's release, post a picture of the cover with its release date. Let the countdown begin!

Including Nonfiction

Recently a Grade 3 class visited the school library and their requests spanned the following topics: Polar Bears, Skate Boarding, Major League Baseball, Dinosaurs, Wild Weather, Baking, Crafts, Science Experiments, Castles, and Mummies. Ensuring that our classroom libraries contain nonfiction is imperative.

- Children are naturally curious and want to know more about our world. Nonfiction is the door to endless information. While capitalizing on students personal interests, it also serves to build their background knowledge.
- At one time nonfiction text was quite expensive to purchase and often written at levels that made it inaccessible for growing readers. Not so anymore! An eruption of stunning, engaging, readable texts has emerged. The layouts, colors, and fonts appeal to students' aesthetic while at the same time broadening student knowledge.
- The majority of what we read and write as adults is nonfiction. Providing our students with opportunities to frequently interact with nonfiction text prepares them for this future.
- Novels require a longer time commitment and must to be read sequentially from beginning to end. The same is not true for nonfiction. The table of contents and index support readers in jumping in and around the text to focus on specific facts. Informational text also tends to be shorter in length, requiring less of a time commitment. It can be set aside and picked up with ease at a later date, which is difficult with fiction.
- Nonfiction topics and titles support our curriculum, especially in science and social studies. Guaranteeing that our classroom libraries contain texts that connect with our curriculum extends the learning for our students.

Release the Students

You may be wondering how to keep track of the books in your collection and about student sign-out procedures. Over the years we've played around with various methods and have found that the best way is the simplest: the honor system. Communicate from day one the importance and value we place on the classroom library, and students will come to treasure the collection and treat books with a high level of respect and care. Each year we do lose a few books, but we choose to believe that those titles have gone to a good home.

Your reading environment is comfortable and cozy—check. You have created a vast and varied classroom library—check. You have scheduled time daily for independent reading—check. Students are savvy selectors and know how to select text—check. Now it's time to go "shopping"! To make certain this experience is efficient and effective, you need to establish routines. Consider designating one day a week as book-shopping day for the entire class. This enables you to be in the library to support all students with book selection. You can have impromptu conversations with students about books they are returning as well as new possibilities. You're also able to remind them about selection practices (e.g., choosing *ACE* books; see page 63), to check in with serial book abandoners, to see which texts are hot items and which need to be highlighted and book-talked, and to make sure that all readers have a variety of text for the week ahead. Shopping once a week avoids unprepared readers, protects sacred reading time, and prevents reading emergencies. Before inviting students to shop, consider setting aside a few minutes for spontaneous book selling. Encourage your readers to sell texts that they think their peers would enjoy before returning them to the shelves. This transfer of books from hand to hand supports and sustains your reading community.

To avoid congestion, invite small groups of students to shop in the library with your support. Keep in mind that shopping in the classroom library is not a Black Friday sale where students cram into the space and randomly grab books off the shelves. They are not elbowing one another out of the way to snatch their next read. Rather, book shopping is structured, thoughtful, and intentional. It is structured: the entire class shops one day a week; a small number of students enter the library at a time and are given support from the teacher with book selection. It is thoughtful: students are reminded, supported, and encouraged to use the savvy selector techniques previously modeled (see page 61) to shop for books; they use their interests and reading goals as a guide. It is intentional: students are expected to select both fiction and nonfiction reading materials for the week, and to be continually working toward a balanced reading diet.

First Book Shop

Students will
- discover the structured, thoughtful, and intentional manner in which they are expected to book shop

Anne

In my early days as a baker I would jump right into a recipe, only to find in the midst of mixing that I didn't have an essential ingredient. There I was, driving to the 24-hour grocery store at 10:30 p.m. to buy cinnamon. Every avid baker knows that before you get out the mixing bowls and measuring cups, you first make sure you have all the ingredients you need for your recipe.

Before students engage in daily independent reading, we want to make sure they are set up for successful reading experiences by having all the reading material they need. To do this we must explicitly and visibly model the process of book shopping in our classroom library. To establish this habit, we encourage you repeat this activity weekly for the first six weeks.

1. Introduce the idea:

   Today I'm going to ask that you watch me closely and intently. I want you to see and hear the thinking I do as I select text for independent reading. As a class we will shop once a week for text. You and I are expected to choose reading material that will sustain us for a week, so one book or magazine is not going to do it. I must select a number of texts for the week ahead. It's important to realize that there may be days when I don't feel like reading fiction. I want to make sure I have a variety of texts at hand so I am never left without reading material. For this reading community, our expectation is that each of us has fiction and nonfiction selections at all times. I am going to use my interests as a reader to guide my selections and the savvy selector techniques to support me. For example I am going to make sure I read the book jacket and the endorsements. I'll even take time to read a few pages to see if it is an ACE book for me; that is, I can read it with Accuracy, Comprehension, and Enjoyment.

2. Consider quantity. Depending on the size of your classroom library and the ratio of fiction to nonfiction materials you have, you may set a specific numerical requirement for readers. For example, in Mary's classroom her expectation is: 1, 1, 1: one magazine, one nonfiction text, and one novel; if students are close to finishing their fiction text, they are expected to also have a standby novel. In Anne's class the expectation is five: three nonfiction and two fiction.
3. Consider age. Depending on the grade and age of the readers you teach, your library collection and reading requirements will vary.
4. Consider additional selections. Students are welcome to add to their stash based on choice. For example: some students may select a picture book they wish to read or one that was previously read aloud. There may be times when students are expected to add to their reading stash due to additional requirement made by you; e.g., when investigating Space in science, each student is expected to have a nonfiction text pertaining to the unit.

Stowing Students' Stashes

We have created the perfect conditions for students to engage in independent reading—we provide the time, space, and materials. Once students have made their book selections for the week the question emerges: Where are they going to stow their stash? This comes down to personal preference, cost, and space. We have seen everything from large freezer bags purchased from the grocery store labeled clearly with the student's name to cloth banker bags that zip up and have a plastic name holder on the front. These are great options for younger grades due to the size and thickness of their reading stacks. Both of these options can easily be stored in desks or cubbies because they are relatively flat and thin. However, when students are reading lengthier novels we need other storage options. Plastic magazine holders and cardboard magazine boxes are great alternatives. Every summer we make the pilgrimage to IKEA with our friend Stephanie Cook to buy cardboard magazine boxes. They are affordable, easy to assemble, and sturdy. Depending on the space available in your classroom, determine the place to store your students' boxes. Window ledges, on top of book shelves, and under the chalkboard ledge are all places our boxes have lived.

Reading Records

People have kept records since time began. Births, deaths, weddings, weather, tragedies, political events—you name it, it has been documented by our ancestors. Our past can be found scribbled in family Bibles, musty diaries, photo albums, and scrapbooks. These primary sources are windows into our past and inform our future. We compel our growing readers to formally document their reading lives in a reading record. This tool becomes evidence of where students have ventured on their reading journey over the course of a school year. Its value and role in a reading community cannot be understated. Reading records are a tool to cultivate readers. They nourish our reading community. Because reading records are used on a weekly basis and serve as a focal point of conversations between teacher and student and reader to reader, they are not seen as busy work. Students know and understand their purpose and value. All it takes is a simple, quick recording of the date, title, author, and genre, a checkmark of whether the text was completed or abandoned, and a rating; see page 113 for a Reading Record chart. This ensures that the reading record is neither tedious nor time-consuming to complete. Readers are encouraged to update their reading record prior to book shopping so they have the pertinent information.

Reasons for Reading Records

Reading Diet Record

If our aim is to ensure that each student has a balanced reading diet (i.e., reads a variety of genres), how do we determine if they are meeting this goal? Reviewing reading records with students during conferences allows us to celebrate genres the students are reading and enjoying while at the same time nudging them to expand their diet.

Documentation of Reading History

Since a reading record is a yearlong record of titles, authors, and genres, it provides students with an overview of their journey as a reader. It illustrates their growth and change over time. Students are able to recall when they discovered a new series, genre, or author. They remember, reminisce, and revisit old friends, stories, and places.

Conversation Starter for Conferences

It is rare for our conferences to not begin with a review of a student reading record. They are windows into the reading life of our student. They provide us with countless pieces of information, such as

- what students have completed (*I see you have just completed* Ghost *by Jason Reynolds. Tell me a little about it.*)
- what they have abandoned (*I see you chose not to complete this book. Can you tell me why? What did you learn about yourself as a reader?*)
- the rating they have given the text (*I noticed you gave this title 4 out of 5 stars. What criteria did you use to make this decision?*)

Usually when we question the speed with which a student has read a text, we are trying to ascertain if they did indeed read the text.

- the length of time between different texts (*I see that you have been reading this book for more than three weeks. I'm wondering if something is getting in the way of your reading.* Or, *I notice you read this text within a week. Tell me how that happened.*)
- if the text matches their ability (*You recently read* Dork Diaries *by Rachel Renee Russell and then read* The Blackthorn Key *by Kevin Sands. Which one was a better* ACE *book for you?)*
- if their reading diet is balanced (*It's clear that historical fiction is a genre you enjoy. I see here that this term you have read 5. I wonder what other genre your next book could be?*)

They can also be used to
- springboard conversations about specific stories and topics (*Your record tells me you have recently read* Half-Truths and Brazen Lies: An Honest Look at Lying *by Kira Vermond. I also read that. Let's grab it off the shelf and take a look at the table of contents. Here's what I really found interesting... What about you?*)
- help recommend titles (*I've noticed that you really have enjoyed reading mysteries. I have a couple of titles that I think you might really enjoy. I recommend...* Or *I see you really have enjoyed Gordon Korman's novel. Did you know he has a new one out?*)

Tool for Goal-Setting

Conversations about reading records serve as a stimulus for ongoing goal-setting for new genres, authors and series, and number of completions.

Reading Identity

As patterns and trends emerge on the reading record, a more complete reader identity emerges. For example, Matthew discovered from his reading record that his favorite genre was clearly fantasy and that as a reader he required action to begin right away or he would abandon a text. Conversely Sabrina discovered that when she got hooked on a series she devoured it and that she was particularly fond of graphic text.

Celebration and Testament

When examining a reading record over a term or a year, students experience a sense of pride and accomplishment. They can easily lose sight of the texts they have read without documenting them and the reading record is a testament to what they have read, who they have met, and where they have been as readers. As students use their reading records as a conversation tool with peers, they bond over shared reading experiences and favorite authors.

Peer Recommendations

There is a powerful shift when students begin to identify themselves as readers who have a role and responsibility in the reading community to recommend texts to fellow readers.

Making Your Reading Record Public

At this point in the book it will come as little surprise that we believe it is vital for you to model and maintain your own reading record. As you make your first entries for the grade-appropriate books you've read, take the time to show students how to accurately complete the reading record form while explaining the purpose behind each section. A point to emphasize is that accurately recording the title and author's name values the author's work and supports us in effectively recommending specific books to others. Note for students that the title of a series is not a book title. You may choose to establish an abbreviated system to use for recording genres. If you do, provide an anchor chart of these short forms. As the lead reader in the class, ensure that your teacher reading record is publicly posted and up to date. Also consider completing a class record of books read together. Post this visibly for reference during class literary discussions.

Ms. Elliott's Reading Record

Date	Title	Author	Genre	Finished / Abandoned	Star Rating
Sept.	Stay Where You Are and Then Leave	John Boyne	Historical Fiction	✓	☆ ☆ ☆ ☆ ☆
Oct.	The Nest	Kenneth Oppel	Mystery	✓	☆ ☆ ☆ ☆ ☆
Oct.	Crenshaw	Katherine Applegate	Fantasy	✓	☆ ☆ ☆ ☆ ☆
Oct.	Audrey	Dan Bar-El	Fantasy	✓	☆ ☆ ☆ ☆ ☆
Nov.	Roller Girl ~ Graphic Novel	Victoria Jamieson	Realistic Fiction	✓	☆ ☆ ☆ ☆ ☆
Nov.	The Marvels	Brian Selznick	Realistic Fiction	✓	☆ ☆ ☆ ☆ ☆
Nov.	Fuzzy Mud	Louis Sachar	Realistic Fiction	✓	☆ ☆ ☆ ☆ ☆
Nov	The Night Gardner	Jonathan Auxier	Realistic Historical Fiction	✓	☆ ☆ ☆ ☆ ☆
Dec.	The Honest Truth	Dan Gemeinhart	Realistic Fiction	✓	★ ★ ★ ★ ☆
Jan	Lost in the Sun	Lisa Graff	Realistic Fiction	✓	★ ★ ★ ★ ☆

Reading Record

______________________'s Reading Record

Date	Title	Author	Genre	*	Star Rating
					☆☆☆☆☆
					☆☆☆☆☆
					☆☆☆☆☆
					☆☆☆☆☆
					☆☆☆☆☆
					☆☆☆☆☆
					☆☆☆☆☆
					☆☆☆☆☆
					☆☆☆☆☆
					☆☆☆☆☆

* Finished: ✓
Abandoned: ×

7

Sixth Step: Nourishing the Will to Read

By adopting the essential steps outlined in the preceding chapters, you've set the foundation for creating a classroom of wilful readers. This took time, effort, and energy on your part. However, we know that just because you plant a seed does not mean it will grow and bloom. We must provide it with sun, water, fertilizer, and space to flourish. Your students need you to be their gardener. Readers will thrive and flourish in an environment that continuously provides them with the essential elements to cultivate their will to read. It's never a one-and-done. It's not an event or a lesson to check off. Cultivating the will to read in developing readers is something we invest in on an ongoing basis all year. Just as we dedicate time to teach the skills of reading each day, we must relish the opportunity to nourish the will to read daily. Let's review the five preceding essential steps for cultivating readers and consider ways you can continue to nourish the will to read in your students.

Sharing Your Reading Life

"You can't catch a cold or a love of books from someone who has neither." (Trelease, 2006) p. 101).

To authentically inspire and motivate students to be readers, you, as their teacher, must be one. Chapter 2 provided you with numerous ways to foster your own reading identity. Your students benefit from a lead reader who incites excitement and passion for reading on a daily basis. Your personal reading life will genuinely enable you to the spread the love and joy for reading you hold. Enthusiasm is contagious! However, your personal life cannot be limited to the newest Margaret Atwood or professional teaching resources. It must contain reading material that is connected and related to the reading abilities of the students in your room. Your students are depending on you to be knowledgeable about genres, books, and authors at their level. Making insightful text recommendations and selling students on books is part of your role as the lead reader and as a member of the reading community. In a vibrant reading classroom, the teacher must share his or her reading life on an ongoing basis. The following activities will support you and your students in making your reading life public.

You Gotta Read

Real readers talks about their reading and share their reading lives with others on an ongoing basis. What better way to support your students in doing that than having them complete a You Gotta Read… Card several times throughout the year? Each card asks students to identify the title, author, and genre of the book, and to write a brief summary and provide a recommendation to other readers. Be sure to model how to write a brief summary of a book without spoilers. Encourage students to reread the back cover of the book as well as the one-line description on the copyright page to assist in drafting their summary. Also show students how to entice other readers with a thoughtful recommendation. Proudly display these cards and an image of the cover for all to see on a bulletin board. Be sure to save these recommendation gems in plastic sleeves in a binder for readers to refer to when looking for books to read in the classroom. See page 82 for the You Gotta Read… Card template.

Book Tweets

Twitter has taken the world by storm. In 140 characters or less we send out messages that convey everything and anything. Let's harness this energy and use this platform to spread the love of the reading. Model for students how to craft a book recommendation in 140 characters. Determine the essential elements of your tweet: title, author, captivating phrases, and the necessary hashtags. A couple of examples:

> Keep calm & read ECHO @pammunezryan. Filled with twists and turns. Heart-warming characters. A magical story #GottaRead

> 5 STARS. Fact & Fiction combined. Heart wrenching tale. Unlikely friends. Out of this world storyline. The Boy in the Striped Pajamas by J. Boyne. #GotToRead!

Have students type up these Tweets and post them prominently in the hall for all to see. If you have a class Twitter account, have each student Tweet their recommendation. If they include the author's Twitter handle in their Tweet they may even get a response—an exciting and unbelievable surprise to students.

Cubby Reading Postcards

If you are lucky enough to have individual student cubbies outside your classroom, consider utilizing this unused space as a book promotion centre. Through the term, have students complete reading postcards that advertise and publicize their life as a reader; see page 128 for a Cubby Reading Postcard template. Along with their name, postcards might include the following information:

- current read
- recommendation
- past favorite
- next read
- favorite author
- favorite series
- favorite genre

These postcards are quick and easy to complete, as well as swiftly perused by others. Including a photo of the student with each postcard provides a connection to the reader.

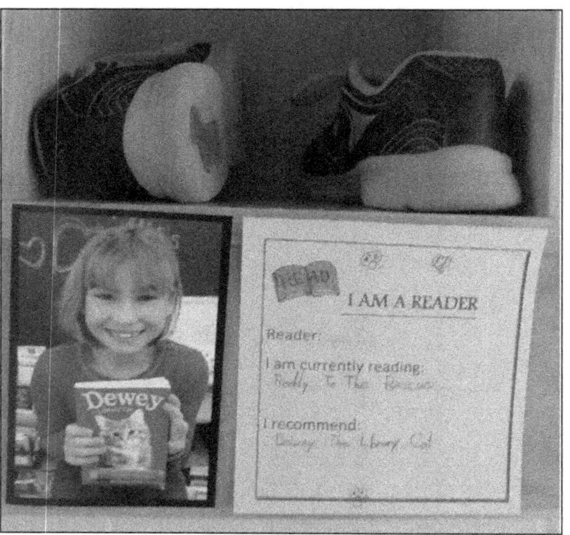

> *Pause and Ponder*
>
> How will you and your students continue to share your reading lives throughout the year?

Knowing Your Students

Readers grow and change over time, so it is vital to frequently reassess and reevaluate the readers in our classrooms. Based on our instruction, the profile of each student will change according to their preferences, habits, behaviors, and needs. It's our responsibility to notice, note, and draw attention to the subtle changes, as well as significant leaps, that readers make in our community. The benefits of knowing your readers abound: it informs your instruction; it fosters the teacher–student reading relationship; it assists you in developing an appropriate classroom library; it enables you to make thoughtful text recommendations; it supports you in connecting readers in your room; it provides valuable data for assessment and evaluation that can be communicated to parents.

Reader Status

Monitoring the status of your readers on a regular basis is important. During independent reading each Monday, check in with your students and ascertain the title and page number of the text they are reading. Using a class list or an at-a-glance chart, quickly record this information. Simply checking in with your reading community each week provides the following information:

- when students have finished a book
- if they have abandoned a text
- the length of time they are taking to read a text
- quick patterns and trends in their reading (e.g., a student who has abandoned their last three choices)
- who you need to have a brief chat with
- facts to inform reading conferences

Genre Graphs

In Chapter 3 we made the case for students having a balanced reading diet. It's our mission to have our developing readers sample from a variety of genres throughout the year. One way for students to monitor their genre choices is to maintain a genre graph (Miller, 2014). At the beginning of the year create a bar graph: the X axis labels identify the genres within your library; the Y axis represents the number of books read. Each time a student completes a text, that information is recorded. This graph allows both students and you to very quickly see a snapshot of each student's reading diet. Also consider creating an abandoned genre tally chart that will allow you and a student to determine if a specific genre has been given a fair shot.

I Used to…, Now I…

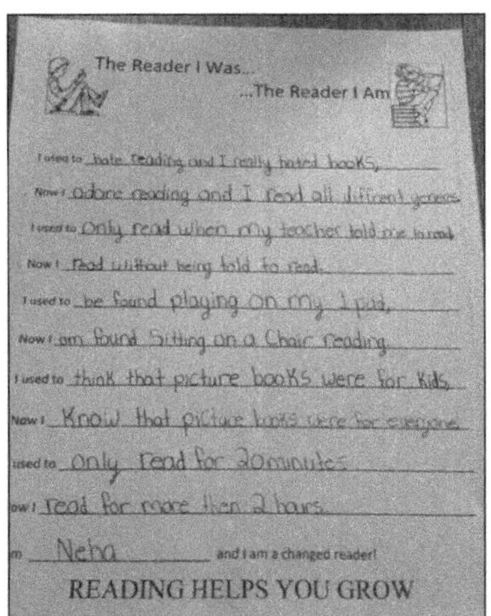

The Reader I Was...
...The Reader I Am

I used to hate reading and I really hated books,
Now I adore reading and I read all different genres
I used to Only read when my teacher told me to read
Now I read without being told to read.
I used to be found playing on my I pad,
Now I am found Sitting on a Chair reading
I used to think that picture books were for Kids.
Now I Know that picture books were for everyone
used to Only read for 20minutes
ow I read for more then 2 hours.
m Neha and I am a changed reader!
READING HELPS YOU GROW

When beginning a weight-loss and fitness journey, you usually start by establishing your baseline: weight, measurements, BMI, stamina, and strength. This is exactly what we ask students to do when we launch our reading community. They are expected to complete a student reader survey and create an I am a Reader Who… poem, as discussed in Chapter 3. Carefully store these artifacts for the sole purpose of dusting them off months later for students to use as a reflection tool. Return these items to each student and encourage them to read over and review the information they reported in the past. Have students consider how they have grown and changed over time. Using the formula "I used to…, Now I…" from *Wishes, Lies, and Dreams: Teaching Children to Write Poetry* (Koch, 2000), model writing your own reader reflection poem. It is incredibly enlightening for students, families, and you to recognize and celebrate each reader's growth. See page 129 for The Reader I Was/The Reader I Am sheet.

> *Pause and Ponder*
>
> How will you purposefully reacquaint yourself with the ever-changing readers in your classroom?

Modeling the Habits of a Reader

In Chapter 4 we identified and discussed the habits of a reader who exhibits the will to read. They plan (what they're going to read, when they're going to read, and where they're going to read), find (purposely select text), act (think about their reading, talk about their reading, and share their reading), and set goals (reading goals that are personalized and specific). All these habits work together to remove reading obstacles and foster the momentum needed to sustain readers. As well, these habits define how we co-construct our reading community, teacher and students together. We set out by intentionally modeling the habits and coach our students as they come to adopt these routines. Providing students with frequent reminders and opportunities to practice Plan, Find, Act, and Set Goals reinforces and strengthens their commitment and the internalization of these habits. These behaviors support students in becoming lifelong, wilful readers.

Planning: Variety is the Spice of Life

If you live in Elgin County, you have been to Shaw's Ice Cream Store on Highway 4. It has been in business since 1948 and the lines in the summer are legendary. One of the benefits of waiting in that long line is the time it permits you to peruse the menu of more than 41 flavors—Grammy's Cupboard, Port Stanley Sunken Treasure, Sweet and Salty Pretzel, Bear Claw, and Country Pumpkin are just a few of their unique and delicious delights. Anne is a creature of habit when going to Shaw's and without fail chooses Mint Chocolate Chip or Black Cherry; Mary is adventurous and seeks out a new flavor each visit. On a recent writing break we went to Shaw's and Mary cajoled Anne into stepping out of her comfort zone and getting a scoop of Polar Eclipse: mint and chocolate ice cream marbled together with cream-filled cookies. It wasn't a drastic change, but a nudge out of her comfort zone nonetheless. And that is what our readers need, a gentle nudge to try a different flavor (genre, author, series). When in reading conferences, take the opportunity to encourage particular students to venture outside their reading preferences and try something new. As well, consider spotlighting specific titles from a genre that is being overlooked.

Planning: Next-Read List

Cream cheese, dill pickles, strawberry jello, sun-dried tomatoes, and bagels—just a few items from Mary's ever-growing grocery list. She quickly jots down what she needs so that she is ready when grocery shopping day arrives. No time is wasted in the store trying to remember that illusive item or making a trip back for a forgotten ingredient. She has set herself up for a successful shop. And isn't that what we want to do for our readers—set them up for successful book shopping experiences? Keeping a Next-Read list is one of the best ways to ensure our developing readers are never without a title to read. Recording the title and author of their future reads on a list is simple and easy, but worthwhile. We have found that each time our reading community holds book talks, we ask that students have their Next-Read lists at the ready. Let the list-making begin!

Finding: Book Shopping Field Trip

Field trips allow us to remove the walls of our classroom and take our students out into the local community to interact authentically with others. These real-world experiences increase the relevance of the work we do in our classrooms. Since we have dedicated countless hours to modeling and scaffolding how to find books, why not put it to the test in a real-world setting? Take your students to your local Chapters, Coles, or independent book store on a field trip. Call ahead to be sure they are prepared for a large crowd, willing to provide a quick tour of the store, and maybe even ready to conduct a book talk or two. Consider asking your principal or Home and School Committee for funds to purchase new hot reads selected by your students while on the trip. Don't forget to remind students to use their savvy selector techniques when making choices.

Our students have access to our classroom library, as well as the school library, but why stop there? Book a visit to your local library for students to get their own library card. During our monthly visits to the Springfield Public Library, librarian Colleen DeVos would enthusiastically welcome the students, read an engaging picture book, and sell readers on new titles. Students looked forward to the change of scenery, a different voice, and access to assorted titles. To set up her students for successful summer reading, Tracy Chisholm took her Grade 7 class to the local library to get their own library cards. Since over the summer students will not have the pleasure of taking out books from the classroom or school library, we have a responsibility to ensure that they have access to quality reading material. Caitlin Moran asserts that "a library in the middle of a community is a cross between an emergency exit, a life raft, and a festival. They are cathedrals of the mind; hospitals of the soul; theme parks of the imagination" (Moran, 2013). And we couldn't agree more. Forging the connection between students and their local library has a variety of benefits:

- It increases the reading community.
- It allows students access to the wealth of knowledge that our society has accumulated.
- Students have the opportunity to interact with another knowledgeable librarian.
- Students become familiar with another way of organizing a library.
- It provides students with access to the various programs and events hosted in their community.

Our local library consistently hosts a Summer Reading Program that encourages a sense of adventure and wonder through reading and engagement in maker activities.

To sustain and nourish our readers, we have to be willing to expand their reading worlds.

Finding: Monthly Top Reads

As your reading community develops and grows, students continue to benefit from support in finding books. The amount of text they are consuming increases, so it is important that they be saturated with possible titles. Adult readers have

Every Sunday morning Mary looks forward to sitting down with the *Sunday Star* while she drinks her cup of coffee to read the book reviews and the top-ten fiction and nonfiction lists for the week. She looks for books that she has read to see if they are on the list and pays particular attention to the titles she has not read. A quick Google of possible next-reads tells her whether this is a book to add to her ever-growing list.

access to multiple sources for their next read, including the bestseller lists, magazine book reviews, and online sources.

Create an age-appropriate monthly list for your readers that celebrates the texts they have enjoyed and are willing to endorse. Using a legal-size page, create a table to record the title, author, genre, and recommender of each text put forth. Be sure to include the name of the month at the top of the page. On the last day of the month, ask each student if they would like to add a title to the Monthly Top Reads chart. Display these charts all year. In our classroom it was exciting to notice particular trends emerging, such as a specific title or author appearing month after month. Honoring student voices and contributions to the reading community this way nurtures our readers.

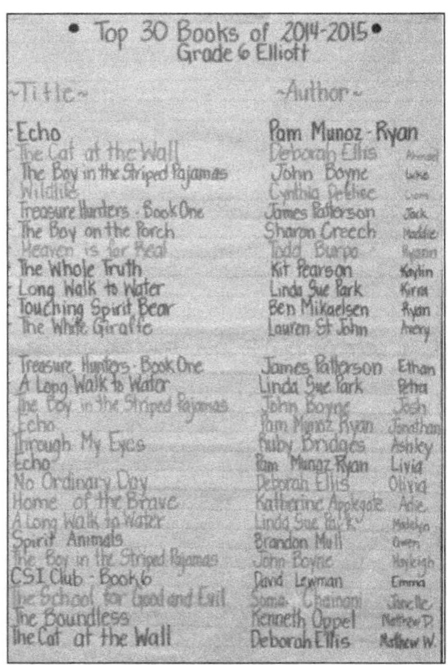

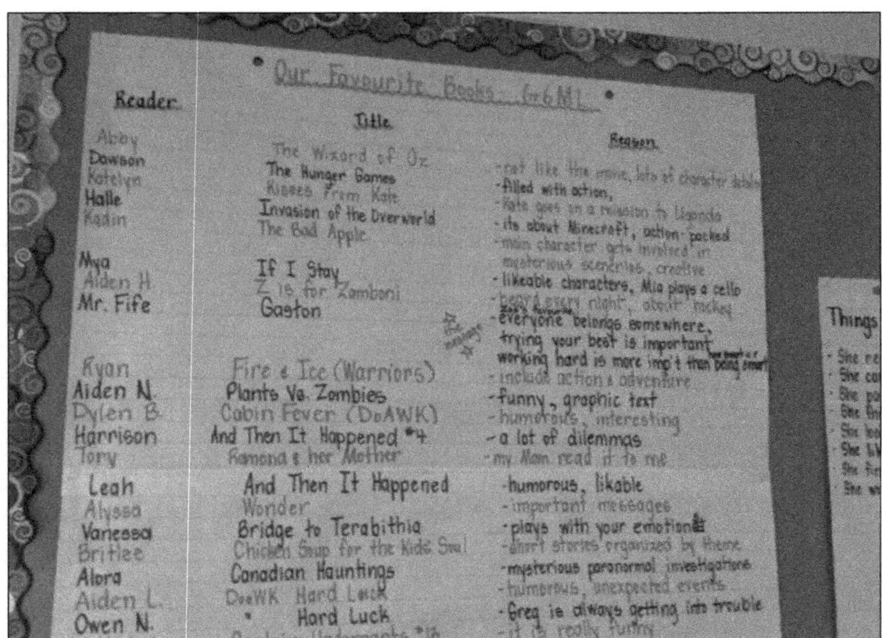

Acting: Characters Written on My Heart

Auggie (*Wonder*), Ivan (*The One and Only Ivan*), Flora (*Flora and Ulysses*), Crenshaw (*Crenshaw*), Castle (*Ghost*), Digby (*Trouble Is a Friend of Mine*), Daniel (*OCDaniel*), Suzy (*The Thing About Jellyfish*)—if you have read any of these books, simply reading the name transports you back into the book and your heart begins to beat for that character. When we connect with a character, we are captivated with their life situation. We may become one with the character and experience their rollercoaster ride of emotions. When they suffer a loss, we cry. When they experience a triumph, we are elated. When they are paralyzed with fear or worry, we read on with trepidation. We never know from where life-altering characters may emerge: a shared reading text, a picture book read-aloud, a fictional novel, a biography. For each reader it is as personal as they are. Be sure to draw attention to the characters we cannot let go of, those who are written on our hearts.

Each term provide an opportunity for students to reflect on characters who have touched their heart. Model for them how to draft a clear explanation for their choice. For example:

A personality that I cannot seem to let go of is a 13-year-old-girl named Hana Brady. Just hearing her name transports me back in time to Nove Mesto in the 1930s. When reading Hana's Suitcase, *I was taken on a suspenseful journey to discover who Hana Brady was and what had happened to her. The love of her family, her steadfast bond with her brother George, her optimism in the moment of despair, and the tragedy of her situation mesmerized me and devastated me. She is written on my heart forever.*

After modeling, distribute templates for students to draft their pieces. We have used heart-shaped cut-outs purchased at the Dollar Store as well as a template with three hearts that allows students to complete one heart for each term; see page 130 for the Characters Written on My Heart template. Make sure to provide the time for students to reminisce and reflect on those memorable characters.

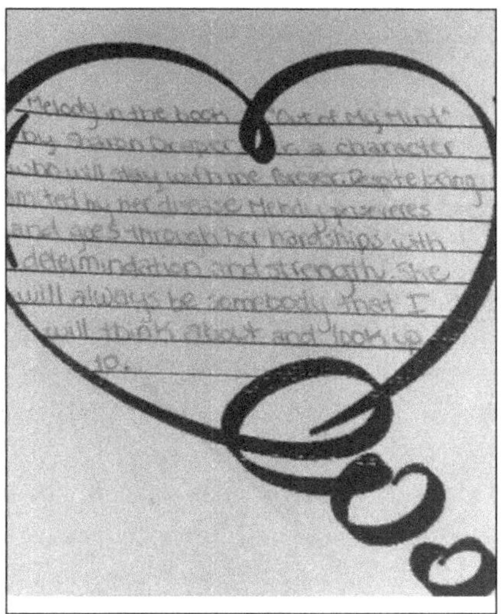

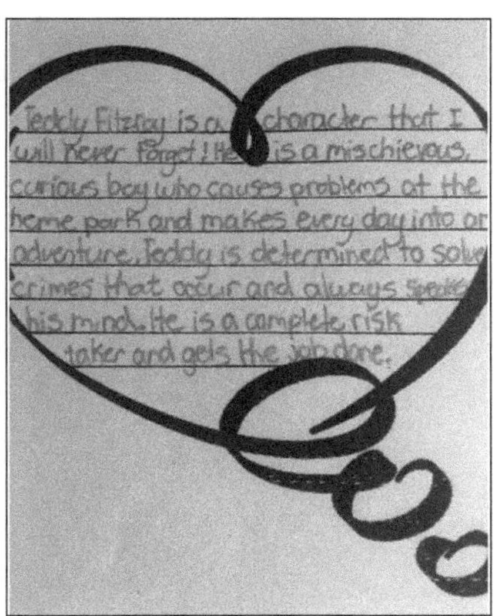

Emma, Jaya, and Braeden, Grade 6

Acting: Reading Passport

Anne has a collection of old passports that she keeps in her Grandmother's antique desk. When she stumbles upon them, she is immediately drawn to the places her feet have trod and the wonders she has seen: Scotland, Italy, Switzerland, Austria, Denmark, and Mexico. The stamps in the passport serve as a reminder of the vacations and trips she has taken. Getting to these destinations required considerable cost and air travel. The beauty of text is that it takes neither. You can travel back in time, into the future, and to fantastical imaginary worlds without leaving the comfort of your couch. Nonfiction can whisk you to the top of Mount Everest or have you swim to the depths of the Great Barrier Reef.

The Reading Passport enables your students to document the significant places they have traveled to through the pages of a book, whether a specific country or a significant landmark in the text. Students may draw an illustration to accompany their brief description. One of the gifts we receive as readers is the ability to travel through time and space, exploring everyday locales and exotic locations, and everywhere in between.

In Dr. Seuss' words, "The more that you read, the more things you will know. The more that you learn, the more places you will go" (1978).

Our reading passport chronicles places we have traveled through the pages of a book:

- an island between Vancouver and Victoria in the 1930s: *The Whole Truth*
- a concentration camp called Outwith during World War II: *The Boy in the Striped Pajamas*
- a farm owned by a Japanese-American family in Southern California during World War II, 1942–1943: *Echo*
- a jungle in Papua New Guinea: *Jungle of Bones*
- a small village in Southern Sudan: *A Long Walk to Water*
- New Orleans during Hurricane Katrina in 2005: *Ninth Ward*
- a small village on the coast of England during World War II: *The War that Saved My Life*
- a run-down estate home in rural England in the 1800s: *The Night Gardener*
- climbing Mt. Ranier: *The Honest Truth*
- America's newest theme park, Fun Jungle in Texas: *Belly Up*
- Germany during World War II: *End of the Line*

Setting Goals: Celebrating Commitment

In our classrooms, students have developed the habit of setting goals, achieving them, and drafting new ones. But we would be remiss if we did not take time to celebrate their accomplishments and growth in frequent and public ways. Validating the time, effort, and energy they have invested in growing as readers needs to be recognized. We're not talking stickers, certificates, or goodie bags, but instead an opportunity for students to monitor and reflect, and for our community to applaud their achievements. Sharing of successes sustains and nourishes our readers. Here are a few ways you can celebrate student reading commitment in manageable and effective ways.

Celebration Circle

Consider facilitating a celebration circle every four to six weeks. Have your readers bring their reading log and/or reading goal bookmark to the circle to orally share. Encourage them to state their goal, identify the concrete actions they took to meet that goal, and any lessons learned. This informal and spontaneous sharing provides momentum for readers to always be striving to become better readers.

Adding Up the Minutes and Books

Time is precious. Each day we honor our promise to students to provide them with independent reading opportunities. They, in turn, pledge at-home reading time and, in their busy lives, are encouraged to look for opportunities to plunder extra moments for reading. Every minute counts and adds up, so let's check in each month and see how many reading minutes we have accumulated. The purpose of this activity is to celebrate the time we have dedicated to our lives as readers, not a measure of accountability. Privately have students total the minutes they have recorded on a pledge card (see template on pages 77–78). Collect the cards and total the minutes to determine the class's total minutes read that month. The next day proudly post the number of minutes, hours, and days your passionate readers have read.

An extension of this activity is for each student to use their reading log to calculate the number of books they have read for the month. Distribute a small sticky note to each student and have them record their name and number books read. The next day, prominently display the total number of books read by the class for the month.

Lessons Learned

In Chapter 2 we explored the effectiveness of students identifying all they know about their teacher as a reader in a show-and-tell activity. During reading conferences, we want students to reflect on their own development, growth, and learning. Initially we support students by sharing our observations and the key attributes we see in them as readers. As we develop a trusting relationship with our readers, they begin to actively contribute their own opinions, reflections, and insights to the conversation. Our guiding prompt is always *What have you learned about yourself as a reader lately?* Depending on the age of your students, record or have them record their key learning on an ongoing Lessons Learned card.

Holiday Reading Challenges

Before each extended break during the school year, have students set a personal reading challenge for themselves that will propel them to reach new heights. For example our challenge card states the following:

> Over the holidays it is my hope that you will carve out time each and every day to get lost in a book and READ! I am asking that you set a personal reading challenge for yourself. It may be about the number of books you want to read, or the genres you want to explore, or even the amount of time you want to commit to reading each day. It's all up to YOU! What matters the most is that you stretch yourself as a reader and increase your competence, confidence, and reading motivation through daily practice.

On the first day back after the holidays, have students use their personal reading challenge to guide their conversation with fellow community members.

Radical Reader Open House

Our partners in education are our parents. It is essential that we welcome them into our learning environment on an ongoing basis so that that they can bear witness to the learning community we have established. Twice a year, students invite their parents to our community to share and articulate their growth as learners. Parents are given guiding questions to facilitate the conversation with their child. Here are a few of the questions we provide our students to highlight their life as a reader:

- What are the unique characteristics of our reading community?
- What are some of the traits of an effective reader?
- Describe yourself as a reader.
- How have you changed as a reader this past year? Explain a few ways you have grown.

- Take out a novel or nonfiction text you are reading from your Independent Reading Box. Share with your parent(s)/guardian(s) how you selected this text. What savvy selector techniques did you use? Explain, *I have chosen to read you a section from this book because...* After you have read, ask your parents to comment on your reading. Did you read with great pace, tone, expression, intonation? Did you attend to punctuation? Did you monitor your comprehension while reading?

To ensure your students have a productive conference, have them practice answering these questions with a partner in advance.

> *Pause and Ponder*
>
> How will you continue to develop the habits of your readers over the course of the year?

Making the *Why* of Reading Visible

Passionate readers can answer the question *Why read?* They are able to provide a variety of reasons why reading is important to them and for them. As a reading community, we have highlighted the following reasons to read: for pleasure and enjoyment, to increase our background and learn more about topics, to become a better writer, to expand our vocabulary, and to learn valuable life lessons. In Chapter 5 we shared activities to provide you and your students with ongoing experiences that illustrate reasons to read. These activities are not intended to be one-and-done, but rather constantly referred to and invested in so that developing readers internalize the will the read. Here are three additional activities to make the *why* of reading visible.

Connecting Our Reading to *Why*

After students have finished reading a text, it's beneficial to have them be metacognitive about their reading. Reflecting on how they have benefited from what they have read, based on the reading reasons, keeps the *why* at the forefront. Understanding the range of reasons that reading is important, valuable, and beneficial to them cements their commitment to reading. Every once in a while during a reading conference, have students respond to the following prompt:

Identify with a check mark which reading reasons you benefited from while reading ______________________________:

- ❑ I derived pleasure and enjoyment.
- ❑ I increased my background and learned more about a topic.
- ❑ It helped me become a better writer.
- ❑ I expanded my vocabulary.
- ❑ I learned a valuable life lesson.

Justify your thinking using specific examples.

Speaker's Corner for Readers

Speaker's Corner was a TV series that aired for 18 years on CityTV in Toronto. This popular show enabled the general public to enter a booth, deposit a dollar, and record a two-minute video on any topic. Segments ran the gamut of rants, editorials, opinion speeches, promotional pieces, music performances, and jokes. This unique forum gave everyday Canadians a public outlet for their thoughts and opinions. Give your students a similar opportunity to make the *why* of reading visible to others by creating their own videos. Provide partners with a tablet and have them select an app that will record their voice and image (e.g., iMovie, Adobe Voice, Green Screen). In the video, students will use the reading reasons to motivate and illustrate the importance of reading to other students. Go public by sharing these videos with other classes and parents. Once you have been bitten by the reading bug, you cannot be silenced. You want to inspire, motivate, and persuade others to read. Let your students do the same.

Author Appreciation

One of our teaching partners and close friends is known for her well-crafted, gracious thank-you notes. Stephanie Cook never misses an opportunity to give her heartfelt thanks to colleagues, friends, and family. In her classroom she shares this lost art with her fortunate students. They come to know how to craft a beautiful thank-you note and the *why* behind the action.

The books that have touched our minds and moved our hearts are truly gifts. The authors of these gems deserve our thanks and praise. Early on in the school year, we purposefully write a thank-you note to an author whose book we have read as a class, typically a read-aloud. We model acknowledging and thanking an author for their story, and sharing how it affected us personally. Sometimes we have been lucky enough to receive a personal response in return. The excitement and thrill this gives growing readers is priceless.

When students genuinely and enthusiastically share their love for a text with you during a conference, encourage them to write their own thank-you note to that author. Provide them with an assortment of thank-you cards to choose from and a special pen to write their sincere appreciation. Author websites and Twitter accounts provide easy access to author contact information. Mail these notes with a return address and hope for a response.

Pause and Ponder

How do you plan to make the *why* of reading visible to your students throughout the year?

Creating the Space

If you wander up to Mary's front porch, you are greeted by seasonal décor, a festive wreath, and comfortable seating. The rocking chairs are adorned with pillows that beckon you to come and stay awhile. For every holiday and season, she changes the color scheme and look to welcome friends and family to her home. This space never appears stale, tired, or dated, but is fresh, vibrant, and current. Mary isn't tearing up the concrete, changing the brick, or installing a new door.

She is just sprucing up the place by making a few subtle changes to catch the eye. When you enter our reading classrooms, you are greeted by a large gathering area, a small-group meeting area, and various reading nooks. Comfortable seating and pillows encourage students to curl up and read. Make certain your reading environment does not become stale, tired, or dated by changing up the space throughout the year in subtle ways that make a strong impact.

Books Come and Go

Our classroom libraries are the backbone of our reading community and feed our readers on a daily basis. As a result we must maintain the collection in various ways to nourish and sustain our readers:

- The texts from our collections are usually treated gently, placed carefully in backpacks, and read with care. But due to frequent use, over time they become tattered and tired. Although these well-loved books have served us well, they rarely appeal to new readers in this condition. So we must invest in newer copies for our libraries. Think about creating a Read to Death bin to house the titles that need to be replaced. This keeps those texts in circulation until newer copies are purchased, and acts as a reminder, when you go shopping or place a Scholastic order, what needs to be on your list.
- There are times when tried and true titles just don't seem to appeal to the students in a given year. It sometimes surprises us that, despite our best sales pitch, we have no takers. Rather than having students sift through titles that it is clear they are not interested in reading, give these books a break and bring them back to the collection at a later date. This provides space to fill the bins with titles that are more tantalizing to current readers (hot authors or popular series).
- On Mary's front porch the accent pieces keep the space current and add an artistic flare. We want our classrooms to be the same—current and eye-catching to our readers. If you change up book displays on a frequent basis, readers are always surrounded by new titles and topics to add to their book bins, and this keeps them keen and motivated to read. Seasonal picture book displays, thematic bins related to curriculum, author spotlights, new arrivals, and award winners are just some of the focus displays we have created in our classrooms.

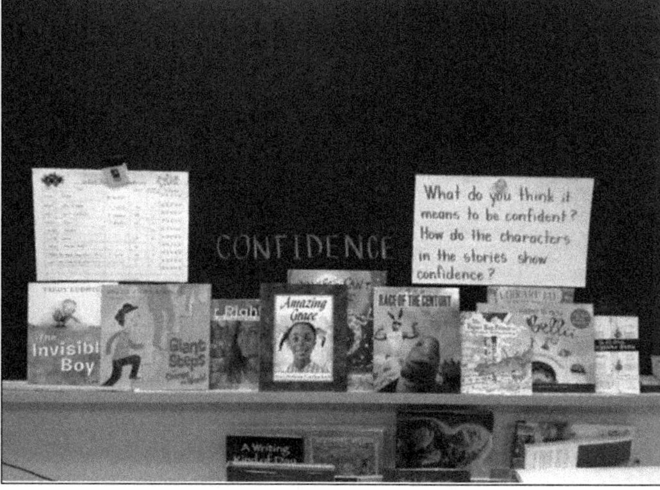

- When students enter our classroom on the first day of school, they are greeted by a vast and varied classroom library. However, the collection does not remain unchanged for the course of the year. It is reviewed, assessed and modified numerous times to meet the changing needs and interest of our readers. As our students' skill and ability improves over the year and as they mature and grow, our collections must change to reflect this growth. Be sure to make modifications to your collection to challenge your changing readers. In addition, when we investigate and discuss sensitive topics, such as refugees, slavery and segregation, residential schools, and the holocaust, our students acquire essential background knowledge and develop an intense interest in these topics. After such experiences, make sure to flood your classroom with appropriate grade-level material related to these issues, including magazine articles, novels, picture books, and nonfiction.

Updating our Book Nooks

When cold winds blow and snow begins to fall, we reach for fuzzy blankets to curl up with while reading. When the temperatures soar and the sun shines bright, we seek a place outdoors to relax and read. Let's create these authentic spaces in our classrooms for our readers. For example, during the winter months Anne provides a few blankets for her readers to snuggle under. A renewed sense of excitement for reading nooks occurs when these inexpensive fleece blankets are introduced. One extra load of laundry a week is little to ask, given the energy and buzz they create. Conversely, in May and June our friend Cara-Rae Clements creates a camping corner, complete with a mini-tent and sleeping bags to sit on, for her younger readers. Or you might ask students to bring a beach towel, hat, and sunglasses to school and head outside. Assigning a specific day of the week, such as Outdoor Wednesdays, ensures everyone is prepared and infuses excitement and energy into the week.

> *Pause and Ponder*
>
> How will you update your space to ensure that it is fresh, vibrant, and current?

Maintaining the Momentum

With the goal of nourishing and sustaining our readers throughout the year, we have revisited each essential step for cultivating wilful readers in this chapter. We hope that the tips and ideas shared for sustaining and maintaining the momentum of your readers inspire you to create your own customized and tailored activities. Cultivating the will to read in developing readers is something we must invest in on an ongoing basis in intentional ways. Naturally, it will take time. Surely, it will take effort. Absolutely, it will take energy. But just like a garden, our readers will not grow, bloom, or mature without a caring and diligent gardener—and that's you!

Cubby Reading Postcard

I AM A READER

Reader:

I am currently reading

I recommend:

I AM A READER

Reader:

I am currently reading

I recommend:

The Reader I Was/The Reader I Am

I used to ______________________________

Now I ______________________________

I used to ______________________________

Now I ______________________________

I used to ______________________________

Now I ______________________________

I used to ______________________________

Now I ______________________________

I used to ______________________________

Now I ______________________________

I am ____________________, and I am a changed reader!

READING HELPS YOU GROW

Characters Written on My Heart

Name: ______________________________

We read to live more lives than we can ever live!

What characters have been written on your heart this year?

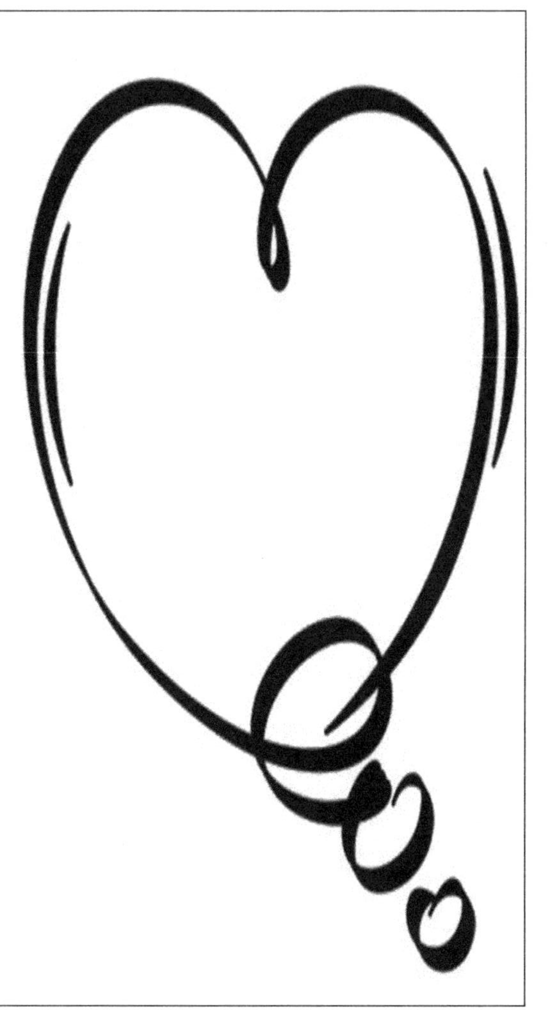

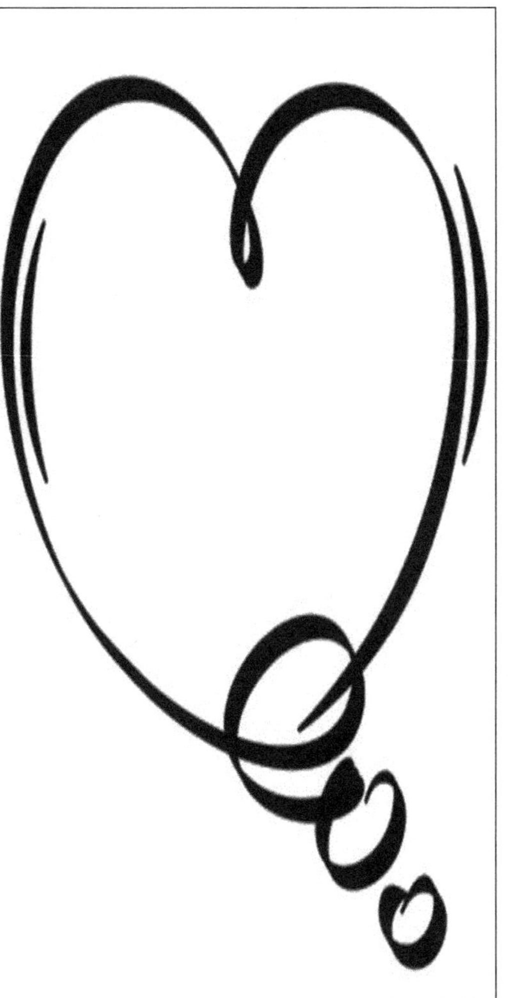

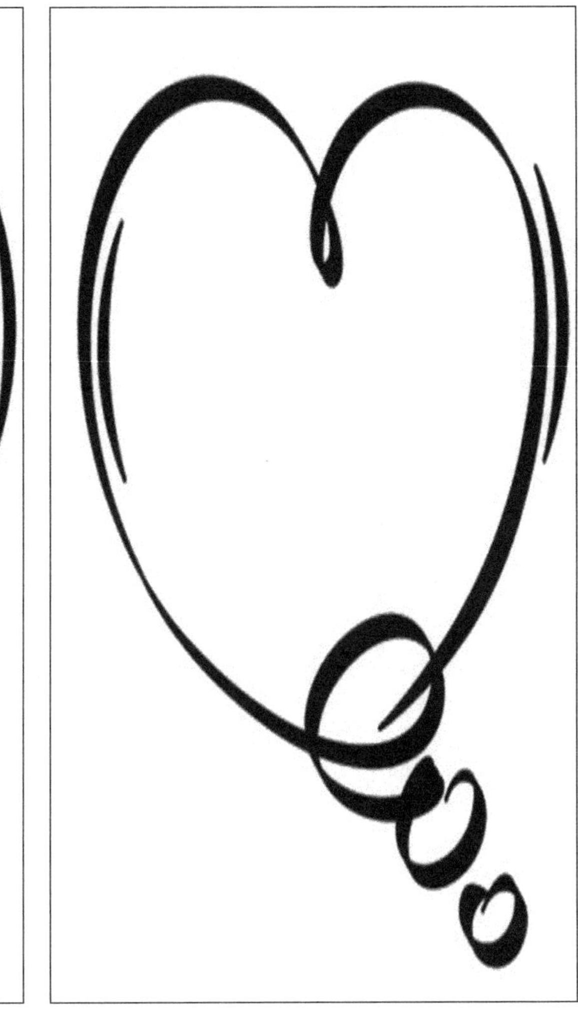

Final Thoughts: Back to the Beginning

Let's start at the very beginning
A very good place to start.
When you read you begin with A-B-C
When you sing you begin with do-re-mi.

— Rodgers and Hammerstein, "Do-Re-Mi" from *The Sound of Music* (1959)

So let's start back at the very beginning—the Introduction. This book began with a call to action by Steven Layne:

> I ask those of you who are truly concerned about reading instruction to become my partners in igniting a passion for reading in schools. I ask you to raise your voices in faculty meetings and college classrooms, in literacy conferences and at parent nights, and educate people about aliteracy—the "invisible liquid seeping through our culture." And then... offer your listeners hope, ideas, and solutions for change." (Layne, 2009, pg. 13)

In *Cultivating Readers* we have offered you our best thinking and work regarding nurturing wilful readers. We are hopeful that our unique response will support you in reflecting and refining your thinking about reading instruction, and that you are filled to the brim with your own ideas for fostering the will to read in your students. Take these ideas, mull them over, tweak them, try them out—and be prepared to be amazed by the transformative power of addressing the will to read in students.

We once heard a speaker say at a conference that, as a teacher, she had a lot of *If-only...* years:

> You know what we mean. *If only* someone had told me. *If only* I had tried that. *If only* I had done that. *If only* I had known that before.

We remember watching countless educators around the room nod their heads in shared agreement. And we too have had a lot of *If-only...* years. What conscientious teacher hasn't?

We wish that, when we started teaching, we knew what we know now:

- that just as important as teaching reading skills is fostering the will
- that I, as the teacher, have a crucial role in creating a community of readers
- that as the lead reader, I can inspire and motivate students to develop the will to read
- that fostering wilful reading requires intentional instruction as outlined in the six essential steps we introduced you to in this book.

Our hope is that after reading *Cultivating Readers* you have fewer *If-only...* years, that you are confident addressing the will to read in your classroom, and that you are supported by the activities outlined in each chapter to create a community of readers. You can indeed teach the will to read if you ground the development of your reading community in these six essential steps.

Acknowledgments

Blessed are those who find joy in the journey. — Anonymous

Journeys start with a single step, but the journey to write this book began with many steps and different roads before it arrived at its final destination. Along the way, we have been blessed with trusted companions whose experience, knowledge, and passion helped us articulate and refine our thinking. Despite the fact that we have never formally met the following gurus, we consider them our travelmates on this journey: Steven Layne, Donalyn Miller, Kelly Gallagher, Penny Kittle, Regie Routman, Stephanie Harvey, Anne Goudvis, Ellin Keene, Debbie Miller, Tanny McGregor, and Cris Tovani. Reading their books, watching their videos, and listening to them speak at conferences cemented our beliefs and inspired us to add our voice to the literacy conversation. But it all began with Charmaine Graves, a literacy legend in Thames Valley. Her vision and direction for our school board transformed literacy instruction and elevated teacher practice to new heights. We admire her intelligence, work ethic, and drive to ensure that all teachers use sound research and pedagogy to inform their instruction. She was instrumental in bringing the two of us together as Literacy Coaches, along with our partner in crime Stephanie Cook. As a Thames Valley Teacher Trio, we have spent countless hours reflecting on our literacy instruction—in cars, on beaches, in living rooms, in backyards, in empty classrooms, in restaurants—you name it and we have lost track of time there talking kids, talking books, and talking practice. Cookie is hands down one of the most gifted educators you will ever have the chance to meet. When watching her interact with children, one cannot help but be captivated and awe-inspired. All of our initial conversations and activities around creating wilful readers began with Stephanie. Where would this book be without her creativity, sense of fun, and note-taking abilities?

In our careers we have been incredibly fortunate to work alongside and learn from talented, ambitious, and innovative educators. Jane Baird, Cara-Rae Clements, Annette Gilbert, and Susan Grieve—all exemplify the characteristics of exceptional teachers. They are the educators you would want to teach your own children. We thank them for inspiring and supporting us throughout this journey. When the road became bumpy and tiresome, they each offered us the encouragement, optimism, and reassurance that we so desperately needed.

This project has required every ounce of our free time, and we cannot thank our families enough for their understanding and patience while we brought this dream to reality. A special thank you to Peter, Mark, and Jennifer Lynch, who tiptoed around the kitchen table for two years while we wrote and rewrote and rewrote this book.

We would be remiss if we did not offer our heartfelt thanks to the countless students we have been honored to work with. Their faces, names, and stories were the catalyst for this book and the motivation to find answers to our questions. They have enriched our teaching lives and we thank them.

Lastly, who would have ever thought that a chance meeting with Mary Macchiusi at The Coffee Pot restaurant in New Orleans during the ILA conference would lead to the publication of this book? We are forever indebted to her for her ongoing interest in our work and the expertise she wielded in shaping this project to fruition. As first-time authors, our sincere appreciation goes out to our conscientious and thoughtful editor Kat Mototsune. She guided us through uncharted waters with grace, patience, and precision. We thank them, and know we are in good hands at Pembroke Publishers.

Professional Resources

Allington, Richard L. (2012) *What really Matters for Struggling Readers: Designing Research-Based Programs, Third Edition.* Boston, MA: Pearson.

— (2012) Summer: Some are reading, Some are not (Slides), American Reading available at https://www.americanreading.com/ documents/Summer.pdf

Atwell, Nancy (1998) *In the Middle: New Understandings About Writing, Reading, and Learning, Second Edition.* Toronto, ON: Irwin.

Beers, Kylene (2003) *When Kids Can't Read: What Teachers Can Do.* Portsmouth, NH: Heinemann.

Bennett, Samantha (2011) "How to Choose a Just Right Book" in Kittle, 2011.

Blauman, Leslie (2011) *The Inside Guide to the Reading-Writing Classroom: Strategies for Extraordinary Teaching.* Portsmouth, NH: Heinemann.

Booth, David (2002) Even Hockey Players Read: Boys, Literacy, and Learning. Markham, ON: Pembroke.

Britton, James N. (1970) *Language and Learning.* Harmondsworth, UK: Penguin Books.

Bromley, Karen (2004) "Rethinking Vocabulary Instruction" *The Language and Literacy Spectrum*, V14, Spring.

Dorfman, Lynne R. & Rose Cappelli (2007) *Mentor Texts: Teaching Children Through Children's Literature, K–6.* Portland, ME: Stenhouse.

Education Quality and Accountability Office (2015–2016) Assessment Reports available at www.eqao.com

Fletcher, Ralph (2010) *Pyrotechnics on the Page: Playful Craft That Sparks Writing.* Portland, ME: Stenhouse.

Fox, Mem (2008) *Reading Magic: Why Reading Aloud to Our Children Will Change Their Lives Forever.* New York, NY: Harcourt, Inc.

Gallagher, Kelly (2004) *Building Adolescent Readers* (Video). Portland, ME: Stenhouse.

— (2003) *Reading Reasons: Motivational Mini-Lessons for Middle and High School.* Portland, ME: Stenhouse.

Gallozzi, Chuck (2009) Benefits of Laughter, Saturday, April 18, Personal-Development.com.

Gambrell, Linda B. (1996) "Creating classroom cultures that foster reading motivation" *The Reading Teacher*, Vol. 50, No. 1, September.
Gear, Adrienne (2015) *Reading Power: Teaching Students to Think While They Read, Revised and Expanded Edition*. Markham, ON: Pembroke.
Hale, Elizabeth (2007) *Crafting Writers, K–6*. Portland, ME: Stenhouse.
Harvey, Stephanie & Anne Goudvis (2007) *Strategies That Work: Teaching Comprehension for Understanding and Engagement, Second Edition*. Portland, ME: Stenhouse.
Irving, John (1998) "It Was 20 Years Ago Today" *Los Angeles Times* (Online), Spring.
Johnson, Pat & Katie Kreier (2010) *Catching Readers Before They Fall: Supporting Readers Who Struggle, K–4*. Portland, ME: Stenhouse.
Keene, Ellin Oliver & Susan Zimmerman (2007) *Mosaic of Thought: The Power of Comprehension Strategy Instruction, Second Edition*. Portsmouth, NH: Heinemann.
Kittle, Penny (2012) *Book Love: Developing Depth, Stamina, and Passion in Adolescent Readers*. Portsmouth, NH: Heinemann.
Koch, Kenneth (2000) *Wishes, Lies, and Dreams: Teaching Children to Write Poetry*. New York, NY: Harper Perennial.
Krashen, Stephen D. (2004) *The Power of Reading: Insights from the Research, Second Edition*. Portsmouth, NH: Heinemann.
Layne, Steven L. (2009) *Igniting a Passion for Reading: Successful Strategies for Building Lifetime Readers*. Portland, ME: Stenhouse.
Luke, Allan (2014) *Reading the World* (Video).
Mandela, Nelson (2003) Address at St. Johns School, Johannesburg, November.
McGregor, Tanny (2007) *Comprehension Connections: Bridges to Strategic Reading*. Portsmouth, NH: Heinemann
Miller, Debbie (2008) *Teaching with Intention: Defining Beliefs, Aligning Practice, Taking Action*. Portland, ME: Stenhouse.
— (2002) *Reading With Meaning: Teaching Comprehension in the Primary Grades*. Portland, ME: Stenhouse.
Miller, Donalyn & Susan Kelley (2014) *Reading in the Wild: The Book Whisperer's Keys to Cultivating Lifelong Reading Habits*. San Francisco, CA: Jossey-Bass.
Miller, Donalyn (2009) *The Book Whisperer: Awakening the Inner Reader in Every Child*. San Francisco, CA : Jossey-Bass.
Moran, Caitlin (2013) "Libraries: Cathedrals of Our Souls" *Huffington Post*, January 9.
Morrow, L. (1983) "Home and school correlates of early interest in literature" in Krashen, 2004.
Paterson, Katherine (1995) *A Sense of Wonder: On Reading and Writing Books for Children*. New York, NY: Penguin.
Pearson, P. David, J. A. Dole, G. G. Duffy & L. R. Roehler (1992) "Developing Expertise in Reading Comprehension: What Should Be Taught and How Should It Be Taught?" in *What Research has to Say to the Teacher of Reading, 2nd edition*. ed. J. Farstup and S.J. Samuels, Newark, DE: International Reading Association.
Pearson, P. David & M.C. Gallagher (1983) "The Instruction of Reading Comprehension" *Contemporary Educational Psychology* 8, 317–344.

People for Education (2011) "Reading for Joy" Toronto, ON: People for Education. Available at www.accessola.org/ola_dev/Documents/OLA/issues/Reading-for-Joy.pdf

Peterson, Shelley Stagg & Larry Swartz (2008) *Good Books Matter: How to Choose and Use Children's Literature to Help Students Grow as Readers.* Markham, ON: Pembroke.

Programme for International Student Assessment (PISA): www.oecd.org/pisa

Rog, Lori Jamison (2011) *Marvelous Minilessons for Teaching Intermediate Writing, Grades 4–6.* Newark, DE: International Reading Association.

Routman, Regie (2003) *Reading Essentials: The Specifics You Need to Teach Reading Well.* Portsmouth, NH: Heinemann.

Scholastic Canada (2017) Kids and Family Reading Report (Online). Available at http://www.scholastic.com/readingreport/

Seuss, Dr. (2003) *I Can Read With My Eyes Shut!* New York, NY: HarperCollins.

Tovani, Cris (2000) *I Read It, But I Don't Get It.* Portland, ME: Stenhouse.

Trelease, Jim (2006) *The Read-Aloud Handbook, Sixth Edition.* New York, NY: Penguin.

Index